Memoirs of a French Courtesan

Volume 2: Spectacle

Memoirs of a French Courtesan

Vol. 2: Spectacle

Céleste Mogador

Translated by Kristen Hall-Geisler

Practical Fox, LLC
Portland, Oregon

Copyright ©2024 Kristen Hall-Geisler

Translation by Kristen Hall-Geisler
Original title: *Memoires de Céleste Mogador*
Translation copyright ©2024 by Practical Fox
All rights reserved

Paperback ISBN: 978-979-8-9903034-0-9
Ebook ISBN: 979-8-9903034-1-6
Mogador, Céleste
Memoirs of a French Courtesan
Volume 2: Spectacle

Neither artificial intelligence nor large language models were used to translate, edit, or design this work.

Practical Fox, LLC
Portland, Oregon
www.practicalfox.com

10.

THE MABILLE BALL

It was nine o'clock in the evening when Marie and I arrived at les Veuves. Mabille was a small ball held in the country, and it was lit with oil lamps. You paid ten sous to enter. It was the where the valets and ladies' maids liked to go in an era when they were at least as elegant as their employers.

Even at this time, Mabille was already gorgeously decorated. It wasn't yet the magnificent garden that you see today, with its baskets of flowers, garlands of firelight, and water fountains, its grand hall trimmed in gold, velvet, and mirrors. It was a modest garden! Gas lamps had replaced some of the oil lamps, but they were rare. Was this due to economy or discretion? The calico workers, the shop girls, and the milliners knew the answer: it was because the regulars had changed.

The ball had already started. We paid a franc to enter.

Marie and I made our entrance as the party was underway. The orchestra, which was very good, was in the center of the garden. My heart began to beat along with the music. I adored music. All the men and all the young girls who work nonstop all week long took Sunday off. They were lively, swimming in sweat, tired, but so undeniably happy.

I had never been dancing. I wanted to try, but the fear of being made fun of held me back. Adolphe had told me that Louisa Aumont was good at the waltz, so I wanted to give it a try. I was asked to dance a quadrille, and I was about to refuse when a young man from Versailles came to wish me a good evening. I accepted that invitation to dance, and I begged Marie to dance opposite me. If my partner had asked what I did, I would have had to injure myself to get out of answering! He was a gentleman, and I paid him a thousand compliments. Then he wanted to waltz with me, and I accepted again since he was so patient with me. That's how I learned to waltz that very evening—to dance at all. I begged my partner's leave to allow me to freshen up.

I took a turn around the ball, stopping at each swirling circle of good dancers. One of these circles had more curious onlookers than the others. I tried to find myself a spot, but no one would budge. I heard laughter, and "Bravo!," but I didn't see anything. I waited until the end to see who had been such a success.

The circle opened up, and everyone surged, laughing and talking, toward a woman. I could only hear the muddled sounds of compliments and teasing. This woman looked at everyone surrounding her. She was probably five feet tall; she was petite, and her bosom bulged. She proudly held her head up, and her hair was a beautiful, gleaming black. She had braids that met in a pigtail at the back of her head, with loose locks falling around her neck. Her forehead was low, and her arched eyebrows met in the middle, which gave her a sharp look. Her large black eyes seemed to look without seeing, her nose was kind of like Roxelane's of the Ottoman Empire, and she had disdainful lips. She was more pretty than ugly, but you probably wouldn't call her cute. My first impression was that she was ugly. I didn't understand why everyone gathered around her like that.

She moved to the side for coffee. I followed her so I could be in the inner circle when she danced again. She seemed out of breath; she coughed, put a hand to her breast, then swallowed two glasses of cold water as if to extinguish the fire that she was holding back with her fingers. She exhaled noisily and stood up.

A short gentleman came over and signaled to her. He was very kind but very droll. He had such a lovely face, including his intelligent eyes. His legs were short, his waist long; he could have worn his jacket as a smock. He windmilled his arm, cocked his hat to one side, lifted his foot to the end of his partner's nose, then bowed all the way to the floor with an arched back. After all these moves, he took her by the waist, and the first bars of the next dance started up.

He was light as a bird. All these steps, which were ridiculous when the others did them, were graceful when he did them. I had to follow these two after the dance was over. There were even more people encircling them than the first time.

At the beginning of the second figure, his partner looked at the orchestra's conductor. Just as the bow struck the strings, she tossed her head low with her arms behind her. Then, at the edge of the circle, she straightened, arched her back so that her elbows almost touched behind her, lifted her head, and stepped forward. She did these contortions with all the seriousness in the world.

"Bravo! Bravo!" said the spectators.

She wore a dress of black wool that spoke of sorrow. She must not have eaten all day, she was so pale.

I heard one of the two young men next to me say, "Bring her some soup!"

"Non," said the other one, "she'll pluck out our eyes from our heads. I heard that she hasn't eaten for a week."

"We'll make her eat," said the first. "She'll humor us."

After the dance, these two men approached her. I heard her accept, so I followed.

Her partner stood next to me. He wiped his forehead and said, "I don't like to dance with her; she's thin as a rail."

They called, "Brididi!"

And this short young man who had danced so well answered, "Here! Here!" and set off for the café.

The ball ended, and Marie and I went home.

※

I hoped, as always, to receive news from Adolphe at Versailles. I asked the doorman if anyone had come by, and he said no. I went to bed and cried.

The following Thursday, I went back to Mabille with Marie. We looked for Brididi and his partner. She was one of the first women I noticed. She wore a dress of lilac gauze, and her hair was better pinned up. She seemed less ugly to me this time.

A man of a certain age with a gray hat, white pants, and a short jacket stopped in front of her. "So we're full of energy again! It doesn't matter; your face is not quite what you'd call beautiful. It has a wild look, like the Queen of Tahiti, Pomaré."

All those who heard him said together, "Chicard is right, we must call her Pomaré!"

When she began to dance, everyone gathered around, and to encourage her, they yelled their heads off: "Bravo! Pomaré!"

That night was an event, and most of the papers ran stories about it the next day. But that evening, M. Brididi didn't seem happy. He danced with pretty girls, but they didn't hold his attention like Pomaré. He decided to give her a rival and looked for someone to serve his purpose. I had looked his way so often that he thought I wanted to dance with him, which was, after all, a great honor. He came over and asked me. I told him I would be glad to, but I didn't know how to dance.

"That's fine, I'll teach you."

And so he escorted me onto the floor. I have a small waist and lovely arms. I took off my shawl and wore only my gauze dress with short sleeves. Many people watched, which encouraged me. I leapt light as a feather!

After the quadrille, Marie, who had held my shawl and hat, said, "You know, you dance very well."

"Certainly," added M. Brididi.

I was so proud! I wanted to be called Pomaré too! I developed a taste for dancing.

At the end of the evening, M. Brididi said to me without warning, "Would you like to come to supper with us?"

I accepted at once, and we left in a merry band to have supper at chez Vachette. I looked around to see if I'd been seen, if this would get back to Versailles. Marie followed along. Her lover was in Brittany, so I had her all to myself. We didn't leave the restaurant until six in the morning.

"Anything for me?" I asked the concierge when I came in.

"Non."

I went upstairs very sad, but I fell asleep without crying. I was too tired.

⁂

At four the next afternoon, M. Brididi came to see us.

"You don't know," he began without even saying hello, "there's a new dance: the polka! Come spend the evening at my place. We'll learn the dance together. It'll enrage Pomaré."

This idea seemed fun enough—not because I hated this woman, but because it was a way to occupy my time.

He and I practiced for five hours. By the end, I knew the polka very well. You take a bunch of steps that make you seem like clever dogs: arms, legs, body, head, all moving at once. You could say it sounded like a telegraph and we looked like puppets. But it was new, and we thought it was fun.

M. Brididi wanted to engage me to stay at his house, but it was too late, and I thanked him. He offered to take me home. He was a charming boy, and I didn't want him to think me a tease, so I told him my heart was spoken for. But I sang the bad news to him and did a polka hop with each phrase.

This made Marie laugh, and she said to M. Brididi, "All right, that's enough. Take care of yourself. I hope you get over her soon."

We arrived at home, and I asked, "Has anyone come?"

"Non."

I stifled a sob deep in my heart.

As we went to my room, I began to polka.

"I'm glad," Marie said, "you took that rather cheerfully."

"That's how it has to be. If I stood there crying, it wouldn't help anything. You can't force people to love you; when you run after them, you just tire them out. They get used to being chased and treat you even worse. Unfortunately, that doesn't erase love from one's heart as if it's a name written on a chalkboard. But with patience, everything passes. I'm giving up hope of making Adolphe love me, but I want him to notice me as I go by, shining and scornful. He'll be sorry."

※

The furniture vendor came to tell me the next day that my rooms were ready. I took my bag and moved into no. 19 rue de Buffaut, on a little mezzanine between two floors.

It was richly furnished, and I looked at all this luxury very worried about how much I had paid. I had a mahogany bed, a vanity table, a Voltaire armchair in red wool, two side chairs, and a small table. In the front room, which served as both entry and dining room, there was a round table and four caned chairs. I spent the day touching my furniture, saying "My home" as I did.

The next day, I went to Marie's. I knew that she was

too lazy to come over.

That night I tied velvet bows in my hair, put on my dress and boots, and went out. I went back to the ball.

Brididi came up to me. I was not upset to see that he preferred me. I read the orchestra's intent: polka! My heart thumped. I became very pale, and I said to Brididi, "I don't dare dance that here. No one knows the polka. They're going to watch us. I'll make some mistake, and they'll make fun of us."

"Non, non," he said. "We'll dance in a corner."

I started to resist, then I heard from behind me, "What, no one knows this dance?"

I recognized the voice of Louisa Aumont.

I took Brididi in my arms and forced him to dance. He was kind enough to say, "You're not on the beat. You're all over the place."

That got me to pay more attention, and I then danced marvelously. We were in front of Louisa Aumont for a while, and I held my partner so tightly that she probably thought we were kissing. He wanted to take a break, but as we neared her again, I called out, "Come on, come on!" He didn't listen.

The crowd applauded as I left the floor. They followed me and pointed.

"The horror," said Louisa Aumont, who was on the arm of an old man. "To show off like that!"

I was well aware that she was irked. All the same, her words pricked at me. I wanted revenge.

I waited until she was passing by me. I reached out to stop her and said, "Hello, my dear Louisa. Has it been long since you've been to Versailles to see your lover?"

She turned crimson and tried to continue on her way. I stopped her again.

She said, "Do I know you?"

"I understand; pardon me. I took monsieur to be your father. If I had known that this was the old owl who bores you so much, the man to whom you say that you're going to your aunt's at Versailles, I wouldn't have spoken of your Henri. But you didn't warn me! You said he was an old monster. I find monsieur very good looking myself."

I curtsied and left laughing.

I began dancing again, and everyone came to watch. I had come to the ball out of spite, and I was radiant. I heard someone say, "She's better than Pomaré!" They left off watching her to come watch me.

"You've got the wind in your sails," Brididi said to me.

All the men asked me to dance.

"It would be easier for me to defend the city of Mogador than my dance partner!" Brididi said, pulling me away by my arm. "Wait," he said loudly, "I'll call you Mogador!"

What happened is silly but true, and it wasn't so long ago, yet people don't remember it. A hundred voices shouted *Long live Mogador!* They threw dozens of flowers into the circle where I was dancing.

There were two camps: on one side, they yelled, "Long live Pomaré!"; on the other, "Long live Mogador!" The people who didn't understand what was going on and only heard the noise yelled, "Long live Pomador!" The doorman had to keep the two camps from mixing. Everyone was so worked up I thought a fight might break out.

I had to escape since they wanted to carry me to my door in triumph. This was a terrifying idea, so, having been tipped off by Brididi, I took flight immediately. Pomaré was put into a carriage. They unhitched the horses, and the young men pulled her all the way to Maison-d'Or.

⁂

The next day—maybe because Mabille had paid to advertise it, maybe because the dance world wanted to make the polka fashionable—all the newspapers wrote about Pomaré and me. *Charivari* had pictures of us doing all the steps. There were two other women who made just as much of a splash over at Chaumière: Maria-la-Polkeuse and Clara Fontaine.

You know what Paris is like. Every oddity has its moment. These lunacies were all anyone could talk about, and our pathetic fame, thanks to the hundred voices of the press, reached the provinces.

I hadn't seen Adolphe for three weeks when he came to Mabille out of curiosity and asked to see the celebrities. He found Pomaré ugly! When someone mentioned me to him, he said, "You're mistaken. That's not Mogador, that's Céleste."

"Oui," said his friend, "Céleste Mogador!"

Adolphe followed me. I saw him, and my legs almost gave out. I pointed him out to Brididi.

"Devil!" he said. "You have to sit down."

Adolphe came up to me. "Come, I have to speak to you."

I signaled to my partner that I'd be right back.

"You will not be coming back," Adolphe said, gripping my arms.

"Why?"

"Because I don't want you to."

"You had long enough to order me around. I warned you that I had changed, and I don't want to listen to you anymore. I want to go dance. I promised."

"Don't go," he said, ashen, "or I will have words with this little gentleman."

I always shook at the idea of causing a fight. I stopped. "Are you doing me the honor of being jealous? It's been some time. I admit that once this would have made me happy once, but now it just makes me laugh."

The flower seller brought me two bouquets of roses and begged me to accept them. I took them, but M. Adolphe threw them on the floor and crushed them.

"Well, then!" I said. "Is your tantrum over?"

"Don't mock me!" he said, beside himself.

I saw that I needed to change my tone, because he was seriously angry. "Come on, my friend. What do you want from me? You left me; you don't love me. I'm not forcing myself on you. I hope that you'll can do the same. I haven't bothered your lovers—"

"I never had that woman! If she were here, I would say so in front of her."

Just then, I saw Louisa Aumont go outside with another woman. "Wait a minute," I said to him, "she's right there! If you do it, I'll believe you."

He hesitated. "You'll leave with me?"

"Oui."

He went right to Louisa, who put on her prettiest smile for him.

"Look, mademoiselle, I beg of you, tell Céleste that I am not your lover and that you're sorry for being so mean to her."

She laughed without answering. He took her by the arm and restated his demand. She scowled fiercely, became red, and said, "Oui."

"Enough," I said to Adolphe, who had clenched his fist. "Come on." And he and I left in a carriage. He paid me a thousand kindnesses, but I sat like a stone.

"I see clearly," he said, "that you no longer love me."

"I don't know if I love you at all anymore, but I definitely love you less. You have no room to criticize me. I loved you; I put myself in a box to please you. And you left me in the most hurtful, humiliating way. I looked for something to distract myself, and I found it. That irritates you. You would have liked me better if I'd shut myself up in a coal box. Good lord, no! You don't love me. Other men are less difficult. It's an embarrassment of riches!"

"You're tormenting me for fun," he said with tears in his eyes.

I was going to relent because I did still love him, but I pushed away the idea of being weak. "Do you think I wasn't tormented while I was on the road from Versailles, on foot and at night, when you let me leave without even worrying about what I would do in my despair? We're not enemies, but I'll never forget that night."

He didn't dare say a word. He loved me, so I was going to be able to get my revenge. I gave him a meeting place, and then I arrived two hours late, pretending not to see that he had been waiting impatiently.

❦

Since I was forbidden, as a courtesan, to go out in public, I made a point of going out. The press continued to report on us at the ball. They came in droves to see us in the evenings, like curious animals. All these onlookers fought over a flower from our bouquets. Women came to see us too; they said to the men who accompanied them, "Make sure that they come speak to you!" They called out to us, but I rarely acknowledged them.

Pomaré watched impudently, causing her to make thousand little mistakes, and the curiosity-seekers fled, red with embarrassment for her. Many came over to compliment me instead.

These are the sordid services that you do for the idle rich. They hide behind anything they can, those who are too old or too boring to be any fun on their own, so they look for distractions, no matter how expensive.

I had my court; Pomaré had hers.

"She is charming," said a man as he ogled me.

"Wait until you see how well she dances," said another.

"What fluidity! How graceful she is!"

This is what they all said, these men who looked down on me, who otherwise found me awful or laughable. But they energized me, and I amused them. Life is a performance.

When I tell you about myself back then and what I think of all the strange things we did, it seems to me that women like me should be forgiven. The attention that created us is more to blame than we ourselves were. The speaker that you admire becomes more impassioned; the actor that you applaud tries twice as hard; the soldier that you watch, that you encourage, becomes braver. There is no creature, whatever position it may occupy, that is not attuned to being in demand. I had no education and had lost everything, so I let myself be dazzled and get carried away. Judge for yourself if I could have done otherwise.

It wasn't only our small scene that had its rivalries, but my success at Mabille brought a lot of envy. Men built me a rampart of love and flowers.

I hated Pomaré, who returned the sentiment. I have no idea why, but people thought it would be fun to have us meet. Our camps negotiated the meeting with all the deliberation of a peace treaty.

We walked toward each other until we were face to face and then took not one step more. She looked at me with her huge, staring black eyes. She seemed more irritated than usual. I wanted to flee, but I realized that would be ridiculous. I took her hand.

She cheered up and said, "I am enchanted to make your acquaintance; I've wanted to for some time. If you would allow me to pay you a visit, I would like to continue my friendship with you."

There was an air of self-preservation about her that put me off, but I took her arm, and we took a turn around the ball together. People pressed in so close that we could hardly walk.

After a bit, I saw that she was taking her role seriously. She really believed herself to be the queen. The fact is, that's the only way people treated her: "Dear queen, are you going to dance? Where will you be so that your court can gather there?" She would tell them quietly, and they would go off, proud and protective, to position their friends.

"Behold! It's Queen Pomaré!" they said as they pushed toward her.

"Where?" said others in surprise.

They pointed her out.

"It's true! She does have a wild look," said a bumpkin who took her for the actual queen of Tahiti.

Once the crowd noticed a regular at the ball wearing glasses—a prefect in a college, I believe. They turned to him and applauded, saying, "Bravo, Pritchard!" The poor man lost his head and did thirty-six leaps. He was carried aloft in triumph. He pushed up his glasses, raised his head, and believed himself a great man. But since they weren't paying him for this display, they sent the poor devil back to his seat. He told Pomaré what had happened, and she said to him—in front me, with all the sang-froid in the world—"Come see me. I'll protect you."

I couldn't keep myself from laughing. I said to myself, *They're each as crazy as the next.* She was convinced of her power. This was the height of insanity, promising to take care of this man. Yet she had an elevated demeanor. I wanted to know this character who seemed to me so strange.

After I moved out, Marie held me to my word. She no longer went home, and I saw her suffer.

At the ball, I asked Pomaré to spend the day with me. She said she only had use of her carriage for four hours, but that in the morning, she would be receiving her court.

"Come to my place for lunch," she said. "We'll chat while smoking cigarettes." She started to walk away, then turned back. "Would you like to have supper with me and some of my friends?"

I said yes before she'd finished her sentence. I really wanted to spend the evening with her.

"I'll take you in my coach."

At the door of the Mabille, she knit her black brows. "Jean! Jean!" she said impatiently.

A kid of twelve came at a run. He was dressed as

if here were in a burlesque: gray pants tucked into his boots, a riding coat whose tails alone would have been enough for a jacket, a very large hat trimmed with braid that glittered as only a costume could. He carried in his arms a cotton shawl, a corner of which dragged on the ground. Pomaré snatched it from his hands, furious.

"Idiot! Pay attention! You're sweeping the pavement with my *cashmere*. If you don't do better, I'll fire you."

Everyone around her laughed, but I became very red. The kid left, shrugging his shoulders, and went toward the coach. It was a caleche with two horses. She'd had it a month. It was almost grotesque, like a cheap rental.

"The queen's carriage!" cried ten kids at once.

Pritchard came forward to kiss her hand. Then she threw coins into the air, and people shoved each other to get to them, crying, "Long live Queen Pomaré!"

The short man sat above the crowd, in the driver's seat, with the same sparkling braid on his hat and a dark riding coat. Add to this scene a white horse and a bay. The carriage was decorated inside with an old, faded red cushion. I didn't know anything about carriages, but I would not have wanted to go out in this one in daylight for anything in the world.

We arrived at Café Anglais. The owner came up to us, towel over his arm, and said affably to Pomaré, "Which room would you like?"

"The grand salon," she said, taking in the size of her entourage.

It had become chilly, so she ordered a fire to be built. When the door of the salon opened, we noticed many heads trying to see us. They lit a small log, and she stood shivering near the fire.

"The first cold snaps are bad," she said to me.

I looked at her. She was pale as death. "Keep your shawl on," I said.

But she didn't. I understood why: she had on a pale-blue taffeta dress that clashed with her shawl. She coughed once or twice, then she picked up a glass of champagne and drank it in one swallow. Her eyes glittered, and her color returned.

Then they made her sing a song, which she said she had composed herself. It was about all the gods from mythology. I didn't really understand it because I don't know all those names, but it seemed to be a masterpiece. Her voice was weak, and she accompanied herself on piano. Her hands were white and well-formed, and they were at home on the keys. She didn't have to look at them while singing for those who listened.

There were endless compliments. They paid very little attention to me, and I think I was a little jealous. She regarded me as if she were the victor.

She spoke, smoked, nodded toward everyone. She had an inexhaustible energy and an unmatched originality.

The night passed. When we left, it was day. These exits are curious, especially to normal people who've never seen this kind of spectacle. The dawn cleared away the foolish fun of the pleasure-seekers of Paris. I don't know exactly what I looked like, but when I looked at the others, I was horrified. The men were sloppy, sometimes wobbly on their feet. The women were sallow, their dresses ragged, their clothes smoky, as if they were walking bags of rags. Even the prettiest were ugly.

Old carriages had spent the night at the curb. A poor, thin horse waited while his master was having his breakfast. Pomaré's court didn't like having to wait, and they called the man names. Poor thing! He was young and blameless. I looked at Pomaré and said, "That's our future!"

At this hour, the only people out were streetsweepers and ragmen. The former see you, lean on their brooms, and say, "What these nuts spend in one night would last me a year." We would give them some money, but usually they passed by without looking at us.

We went home on foot. Pomaré seemed less tired than everyone else. She was extremely pale, but her lips were still red, her eyes still shining.

We crossed the boulevard. A female streetsweeper (there were a few) worked busily, sweeping all the dust onto Pomaré's legs. Being a little brash by nature, Pomaré stopped and called her stupid.

The woman took up her broom and started sweeping again. "Do you see this?" she said. "The lady embarrasses her! Must I stop my work to make room for this young thing? With all her beauty! I've been a little better than you, my dear, and a little more posh, but I was not too proud for the poor of the world." We were already far past her.

We went our separate ways soon after.

"See you soon!" said Pomaré. "No. 19 rue Gaillon. If you forget the number, ask anyone in the street for Queen Pomaré."

I found this unlikely to work. It seemed to me more prudent to remember the number and street.

I had seen a slice of this life that from afar looked so beautiful, a life that I'd so often dreamed of being part of. I could also see that in all honesty, this joy would bring me sadness. I went back to my house with an empty heart and a very discouraged soul.

ll.

Queen Pomaré

AT ELEVEN O'CLOCK, I WAS at my new friend Pomaré's house. I had been expecting to see a richly furnished boudoir, so I was very surprised to find myself in a rat's nest. These weren't so much the home of Pomaré as much as they were the home of disorderly filth.

She lived in a large, fully furnished room. Her vanity table was covered with a jumble of small objects recalling her triumphs at the Mabille ball. Each object had a layer of dust. You could see papers in disarray on a table and a pile of issues of *Charivair*. Her blue dress was half on the floor.

I noted a nice plaster Virgin hanging on the wall with a little necklace and crown. The Virgin, with her arms spread wide, seemed to contemplate this disorder and take pity. Above the fireplace, the queen had set her hat on a platter.

I didn't dare take a step. She was still in bed, head bare and hair disheveled.

"Sorry," she said, "my rooms are not yet done. The person who rented it to me charges too much and doesn't do anything. Have a seat!" She directed me with a look to edge of her bed.

I came over, but I was irritated. She leapt from the end of the bed and went into a small room with a window over the courtyard. From there, she called to her porter, who was also her landlord. He came up.

"Make us lunch."

"Happy to, but give me the money for it."

"I don't have any."

"Bah!" said the old man. "You have at least twenty sous."

"Non," she said, "not a cent."

"Then go out and eat wherever you like. I'm not giving you any more credit."

"Come on, don't be cheap! I invited a friend. I can't send her away."

"Great!" said the old man. "There's not enough to cover you, and now I have to feed others." And he went downstairs grumbling.

I had heard everything, and I was enormously embarrassed. She told me when she came back into the room that we would be eating out because her servant had not returned. The concierge had come to inform her of this.

It was too much. I pressed my lips together so as not to burst out laughing. I had seen her, the day before, toss at least ten francs in the air. Apparently she was a fool.

"I had forgotten you," she said as she passed by the

little Virgin. She took hold of her, kissed her, and said some words that resembled a prayer. I heard the words "Saint Mary of God, have mercy on him; he is happier near you."

She put the Virgin back in her place and came over to me. The movement of her arms made her blouse open. I saw a scapular, medallions, and a small cross against her breast. This made me angry. I have a strong belief in God. When I suffer, I call on him; when I am happy, I thank him. But these Christian symbols seemed like blasphemy against her chest.

I asked Pomaré to wait for me. I went downstairs for a few minutes, and I returned with all that we needed for lunch.

"I'm going to pay you back as soon as possible for all you've spent," she said with incredible tact.

God! This awful woman, I said to myself. *She lies like everyone else.*

I asked her two or three questions about her life before becoming Pomaré. She redirected the conversation without answering me. I asked again during lunch; same silence. Still, I wanted to know what she had been, because everyone was so intrigued.

"All right," she said after lunch. "You are a good girl. Promise you won't say anything to anyone, and I'll tell you everything."

I promised. She began.

The Story of Pomaré
I came into the world in Paris 1825. My father was rich, and I was his first child. He was worth about 150,000 francs. These 150,000 francs were invested in a theater,

and it earned fifteen, sometimes twenty percent. He didn't spare any expense on my upbringing. I was put in one of the first boarding schools in Paris. I had the best teachers. My mother gave me two brothers and two sisters, yet they didn't subtract a cent from what they spent on me.

When I was seventeen, they thought I should marry, but they couldn't find anyone suitable. I loved my father with all my heart while at the same time fearing him very much. My mother didn't make him very happy.

One day I heard at school that an awful fire had done extensive damage to the theater disctrcit on rue du Temple. We were assured that no one had died, but also that nothing was saved. This made me sad, but I didn't think for a second that this misfortune would touch me.

Two days later, my father came to see me. He had always been tall and strong, and I was frightened by the change I saw in him. He was curled in on himself, and his eyes were red. He had been crying. I threw my arms around his neck and covered him with kisses.

"My father, my dear father, what happened? My mother! My brothers! My sisters!"

"By the grace of God, they are well," he said, "but I am ruined. The fire devoured everything. I was not insured. My children! My poor Lise!" He clutched me in his arms.

I had never seen my father cry. This broke my heart. I was very pious, and I had often spoken of my wish to enter a convent, but I had been mocked for it, so I didn't bring it up anymore. The idea came back to me that day.

As I wiped my father's eyes, I said, "Don't worry about me, my dear father. You know that my greatest wish is to be a nun. You won't have to bother with me."

"Non, my child," he said, holding me against his heart. "You cannot belong entirely to God. I need you to raise your brothers and sisters. You've had instruction; you will educate them. Your mother is almost numb with sorrow. She needs comfort and help. I came to get you."

I followed my father out without responding. You never talk back to my father.

Back at our house, I found everyone in despair. My father kept going out in search of business ideas to try. My mother had lost her mind a little. I took care of the children.

Soon we were so poor that they got rid of the maid. It fell to me to do everything on my own. They hadn't raised me that way, so it exhausted me. I was always alone with the children. I took the smallest one for walks.

A young man who my father had employed came often to the house. He told me he loved me, and he tormented me so much that I believed I loved him. I gave myself to him without much resistance. I didn't understand the danger of such a terrible deal at all.

One day, my father came home while I was chatting at the door with my love. My father asked him to not visit me without my mother or himself being present.

My mother often went to see her parents. One particular day, she didn't return at the usual time. My father waited, and she finally came in at ten o'clock.

"There you are, madame!" he said to her severely. "Go to your room, Lise."

I obeyed, but I listened at the door because, knowing the mistakes I'd made, I was afraid of what would happen.

"What is going on with you?" my mother asked him.

"You don't keep track of your daughters," he

answered. "You're going right, then left, without stopping. Your oldest daughter is seventeen, the second fourteen, the last five. The fall of the oldest will drag down the others. If another bad apple like him comes along to deliver another blow so that my despair can be joined by dishonor, I'll kill the bastard who would sully my name, and then I'll kill myself. And that would be on you."

My mother didn't say a word, but I made myself scarce. I hid my head under my pillow to cry, but I still only knew half of the trouble to come.

For some time, I felt ill, weak. I attributed this to anxiety about what I'd done. There was a doctor in our building, so I went upstairs to tell him how I was feeling.

He looked at me and said, "You're pregnant. It's not dangerous."

I made him repeat it twice. I didn't dare tell him to keep my secret. I went downstairs and resolved to throw myself in the river when night came. I ran to the house of the boy who'd brought me low. He only had one way to rescue me: abort the child. I looked at him in horror. I couldn't hate this man enough.

"The very idea will bring you regret!" I said to him as I left.

I went back to my father's house. He seemed to be able to read everything as if it were written across my forehead.

I went to my bedroom to write. I saw my sainted Virgin, and I asked her forgiveness for the thought of suicide. I promised to live for my punishment and for the poor little creature that I carried.

I packed up my things, hugged my brothers and sisters, and left in desperation. I didn't dare turn back.

I thought I heard my father's footsteps behind me. I walked, or sometimes ran, for a long time.

Eventually I came to a beautiful garden; it turned out to be Luxembourg. I went along a small, narrow, deserted street until I saw a sign: Furnished Rooms. I introduced myself to the mistress of the house and asked for a small room. She didn't want to rent to me; of course, I didn't have any money. I told this woman my situation, and I begged so much that she ended up relenting. She seemed most touched when I assured her that I wouldn't be staying long in her house because I was going to go to a hospital to give birth. I was put in the attic.

I asked where women were received for childbirth and was directed to Maternité. When I went there, they told me they only took in women two weeks before giving birth. What could I do until then? I wasn't even three months pregnant; how would I wait another six months? I thought again of suicide, and I fervently prayed to God to take away my life.

I sold off all my things little by little. When I had nothing left, I asked for work in the house. They had me change linens and help with housekeeping. There were a lot of student boarders. I was nice; at least, that's what the lodgers told me.

The woman who ran the house was stingy. She made me work fifteen hours a day for a piece of bread. I had a huge appetite, so I made sure to have a meal at one place, lunch at another. It was an awful existence, my dear Céleste!

It was winter, and cold. One of the young men took pity on me and gave me a blanket from his bed. I fell ill and didn't leave my attic. The same young man who had given me the blanket brought me some little bits of food that he'd taken from the dining room. I was often starving, yet I didn't dare complain. I was afraid of being kicked out.

The day of my delivery was approaching, so I went to Maternité. I was thin and exhausted. They asked if I would keep my child. This question made no sense to me. How could they ask a mother if she would keep her child?

After immense pain, I gave birth to a boy. I asked God for forgiveness for his birth. I prayed he would protect the child's life and take mine. He was so delicate, the poor angel, that I constantly listened for his breath. They wanted to keep me from breastfeeding him, but I didn't pay them any attention.

When the time came to leave Maternité, they gave me a little money and the necessities for the baby, and I left with my treasure in my arms.

I went back to the hotel, and I wasn't received too badly. I took my hole in the wall again, and I worked a little. My poor infant was very pale. At ten months he smiled at me, and I held his little hands. I found myself very happy. I didn't deserve this kind of luck, and it was cut short.

Seizures—every mother's nightmare—seizures put the life of my child in danger.

I clutched him against my heart. His little limbs twisted, and his face turned blue. I covered him in kisses, I warmed him with my breath, I said to him with my hands clasped, "Please stop. Your crying is going to kill me." And I prayed. He relaxed and was quiet for a few hours, then the convulsions returned, even worse this time.

Eight hours passed during this terrifying fight. He

would have an attack, then relax. I thought he was resting. I begged the Virgin Mother to end his suffering by saving his life or taking mine rather than torturing him so. I didn't have the strength to watch him suffer.

I waited a long time for him to wake up again. I lifted him up. He was stiff and cold. I let him fall back onto the bed, then I took him up into my arms again, unable to shed a tear.

You wicked person, I said to myself, *you killed him. Did your prayers even reach heaven?*

I ran to the stairway, calling out that I needed a doctor, that my child couldn't be dead unless I was too.

They came to take the body of this poor little angel from me. One of the young men of the house paid the fees for the burial. I followed my son to Montparnasse. I had them put a marker on his burial so I would know it from the common grave when I had the funds to buy him a cross and wreath.

I spent the next two weeks desperate and insane. I no longer went up to the room where he'd died. Someone let me stay with them.

"Come on," said a strong boy, "you can't live like this. You'll end up destroying yourself."

They made me eat dinner and drink, and they brought me to Mabille.

That was the first time that you saw me, in the black wool dress. I needed money to go back to Montparnasse. I have it, and I'm glad. I'm only afraid of one thing anymore: running into my father again. He would kill me. I've developed an enormous taste for life, and I'm proud of myself. It won't be long before I'm rich. I already have the clothes.

She had recited all this to me beautifully and without a break. She spoke in her natural voice and with true emotion. At this moment I formed a different opinion of her than I had on first meeting her. Queen Pomaré disappeared, and in her place I saw a poor girl even worse off than me. It wasn't until I heard her sweet name, Lise, that I found some kind of mysterious sympathy. When you don't have a family, you make one with the down-and-out and the friends who cross your path.

I took some time away from Lise, convinced that she had bouts of madness. But I felt that I'd developed a great appreciation for her.

❦

My liaison with Adolphe cooled more each day. The first time he'd scorned me had killed my love for him, and the zest that he had shown in his feelings for me since then wasn't enough to rekindle my passion.

Adolphe was far from being boorish. He had spirit—he was bold with his sword and a little quick to anger, but he was light in love. He didn't have the heart for feverish passion or the charm to captivate a woman who'd been thrown into the whirlwind where I found myself.

My visits to Versailles became more and more rare. He tried for some time to fight the progress of my indifference. When he realized that he didn't have enough money, he made a decision he'd been hesitant to make before this point: he took a promotion. He became a surgeon in a regiment that was leaving Paris.

My friends consoled me through his absence. I was happiest in Lise's company; her fantastic intelligence was truly something to behold. Yet she had one huge drawback: she was bonded to a short woman who I learned was called Rose Pompon.

This little woman had a charming face and an awful demeanor. She spoke with bad grammar and interrupted people, spit on your face while she talked, and dressed like a twig. She was stingy—so stingy she'd shave an egg.

Judge for yourself: she got pregnant, so Pomaré took her to a doctor, set up the child's baptism, and bought the necessities. Pomaré sold her own things to help Pompon. Pomaré herself didn't have any money, and Pompon said she was out of funds. Soon after, Pompon left for about ten days. While she was gone, Pomaré was looking for something in a drawer, and what did she find hidden in the bottom? Ten gold louis and some jewelry that Pompon had carefully kept in reserve.

I didn't like this woman, to the point that I went for some time without seeing Lise. The summer balls were closed, and I didn't see anyone anymore. Then I heard Pomaré was going to dance the polka at the Palais-Royal.

My friends insisted I capitalize on the success I'd had at Mabille. They told me that there was maybe more work to be had if I positioned myself as a dancer. The moment had come for me to have another go at working in the theater.

12.

Queen Pomaré Continued

I WAS TAKEN TO BONMARCHAIS, where I was enthusiastically received when I said that I would use the name Mogador.

I was hired. I performed again in a revue the next day, where I played myself and danced a mazurka at the end. My costume was delicious. My debut was the same evening as Pomaré's, and I was very successful.

I learned the next day that Pomaré had whistled when she read the over-the-top responses. Some newspapers that I read had written overwhelmingly bad, mocking reviews. The journalists treated women like governments: They created them; after creating them, they sang their praises; after singing their praises, they wanted to bring them down. If these women defended their reputations—which are their livelihood—the journalists unleashed themselves, insulted them, scorned them. They screamed about depravity. But, gentlemen, if this depravity that frightens you so much has gotten this far, it's at least a little bit your fault.

Back then, there were only one or two public balls. Why are there ten today? Because the celebrities that entertain you create a fantasy for you. This glittering glory causes envy, and thousands of young girls are led into the public balls by the lure of this shiny lie. They'll do anything in the world so that someone might pay attention to them and you might say their names.

Men of good families come to see combat, these barrages of high-kicking legs. How do you expect them to not lose their minds among these young girls, some of whom are indeed charming? They all get drunk together on the same madness.

Pomaré had a carriage. Everyone wanted to have one, and many did. Every day, the Champs-Elysées had ten new elegant, well-crafted carriages with women inside. This luxury was hard to witness, I confess, when you think that many of these impeccable women were wallowing in misery or on the outs with their families.

The vaudevillians and actors, all of whom were able to successfully exploit their sharp passions, put prostitution on the stage. All of Paris sat rapt during two hundred performances of a courtesan's selfless baring of her heart and her agony. Then, one fine day, they became afraid of the path they'd gone down. The civilized world reacted as if it were a virtuous society. Some vaudevillians and other actors, aware of this new trend, hung the rest of us on the scaffold of opinion. Journalists did the same thing without remembering that not long before, they had beat the drum at the door of the Ranelagh, at the door of the

Mabille, at the door of the Asnières ball.

In the great things as in the small, in the honest things as in the shameful, the human spirit is always the same: spinning like a weathervane on top of a house.

If they really want to destroy the power of the high-class courtesans who have a hand in everything, who start within the highest spheres of society and end among the lowest ranks, the way would be to study the facts. The true stories of women who came into this hellish life would be more effective at turning young girls away than the touching idylls and contrasting comeuppances tjat so amuse the Parisian public as it cries and laughs in turn.

Since I lived within this whirlwind, I didn't have time to reflect at all—not on my misfortune, not on others'. Now that I've retired from this scene, when I envision my own disenchantment and recall how the most brilliant and adored women ended up, it seems to me that if you could show them their future in a dream (as in the play *Victorine*), all would turn back from this path.

※

Pomaré became depressed; I had to see her. She lived at no. 25 rue de la Michodière, on the mezzanine. The house had furnished rooms and was decorated very nicely. Lise herself was rather elegant. I listened while she told me of her debut. She didn't think the criticism was fair and asked me to share mine.

"Well," I told her, "it's a start."

"Ah!" she said, laughing. "My start looks lovely from a certain angle. At the Palais-Royal, I had the kind of success Lola-Montès had. There were noisemakers with holes, and you blew into them. The noise drowned out the orchestra. I danced off-beat. It was time for me to flee, because they were about to throw branches at my head. I'm sick again; I won't go out for six months."

"Apart from that, you're happy?" I said.

"Oui," she said. "Look." She opened an armoire and showed me a pile of cloth, which I eyed, I admit, with a kind of envy. "I'm fine. I live with a young man from Toulouse who adores me and fills me up. He works for the post to make his parents happy. They want him to have a job—which he doesn't need. He's very rich."

"Wonderful! I'm so glad. I love you very much, and I'd like to see you manage your health and finances a little better."

"I don't have long to live. I want to have fun and regret nothing. Are you onstage tonight?" she said as she opened the window.

"Oui, every night."

"Good! I'll come see you with my *husband*."

I left her. I saw her again that evening in a box seat on the floor with a short man who had messy blond hair and glasses. He seemed to give her all his attention.

She asked me to dine with them the next day. She told me, before he arrived, that she didn't want him to suffer, but he loved her so much that she pitied him.

Actually, he interested me. He had such an honest, kind personality, and he spoke so lovingly, that I was enchanted by him. I made Lise promise to treat him better.

"You see, mademoiselle," he said to me that night as he drove me home, "right now I cannot do all that I would like for her. But I'm going to have a lot of money from a property that I sold, and I'll give it all to her."

A few days later, I heard in the theater's foyer that Queen Pomaré had been arrested as an accomplice in a massive theft. They were still looking for whoever had planned it.

I couldn't believe it. Besides, I could never stand by and listen while anyone spoke badly of my friends. I denied everything to these vipers, who didn't like me and were delighted by making me worry.

An old chaperone who, unlike the rest, had been very kind to me, said, "My word! Jumpers like that, they do all the work."

"If I were the judge," said an ingenue of about thirty, "I would condemn her to prison for the rest of her life." There's nothing as nasty as being holier-than-thou. This one was so dried up, so ugly, that I'm not going to say any more about her.

"You'd have to put all the even slightly pretty women in prison," I said. "Then there'd be a shortage, and maybe you could get stage time."

"Stop now," one of my friends said to me. "Don't argue without knowing who you're arguing with. You could get into trouble."

As soon as the show was over, I ran to rue de Michodière. The mistress of the house told me that they'd taken Pomaré away in secret, but that she would tell me everything. I was probably at least her hundredth confidante.

Pomaré's Arrest

Yesterday, a man came, well dressed, who asked me which room Mlle. Lise lived in and how she lived. I thought it was her father, who she's afraid of, and I told the gentleman that I did not know her manner of living.

"She's in hiding," he said "Proof that she's guilty." He signaled to two other gentlemen, who also entered, and all three went up to her door, signaling for me to follow. I could tell they were policemen.

"Knock," the man said to me. "She must not be afraid to open the door. Paper can be quickly burned."

I did what they said. Lise opened the door in her chemise. On seeing all of us, she tried to shut the door again, but she didn't have time. The three men entered, one on either side of her, to keep her from moving. The poor girl was so pale that it broke my heart.

"Get dressed," said one of the men while the others went through her drawers and took papers. "You're coming with us."

"Coming with you!" Lise said. "Where?"

"Not to Mabille," said the man. "To the police station."

"To the police station! Me! But what have I done?"

"If you were only dancing, you would only have hurt your legs."

"But monsieur, I didn't hurt anyone."

"That's for the judge to decide. Hurry up; we're waiting."

"A judge! You're arresting me like a thief?"

"An accomplice," said the man. "Same thing."

"Me!" she cried again, raking both her hands through her disheveled hair. "And you thought you could bring me in alive?"

She hurled herself into the next room, where undoubtedly she intended to pick up a knife. But they grabbed her before she had opened the drawer.

You see, Mademoiselle Céleste, this scene badly frightened me. Her hair was a mess, and she was nearly naked because she had opened the door in the middle of getting dressed. They held her as gently as possible. She threw herself to the ground and hit her head; I thought she was insane! Seeing her despair, they began to treat her more kindly.

"Let's go, my child," said one of the men. "Don't get so worked up. Maybe they won't do anything to you. If you aren't guilty, you'll be back here soon. Let's go, let's go, don't make any noise and no one will know. You've taken up with people you don't know very well, who fool you with their resources, with their mere existence."

The three men lifted her from the ground and put her in an armchair. Her eyes were glazed over, and she seemed not to hear. She got up as if with renewed resolve, then she got dressed silently, with dry eyes. Every one of her movements was tracked. She asked me if monsieur had come.

"Non," I said, "I haven't seen him."

"Everyone abandons me! Let's go, I'm ready. Trash that I am! Look what my life has led to. I wish that all those who followed in my footsteps could see me now."

They went to a coach. These gentlemen took her by the arms and placed her in the carriage. I saw her throw her head back, and then the carriage left.

The brave woman didn't know any more. The information that she could give me stopped there.

I didn't change my mind after what I'd learned. I still didn't have a second of doubt that Lise was innocent. I knew she was incapable of a criminal act.

I went for a walk to absorb the news, but I had to be prudent because I myself was under surveillance, which worried me. My involvement in an affair of this kind could cost me dearly. Lise's predicament was a secret, and nothing could make me rat her out.

I went back to her house twenty times. I couldn't shake off the blow that her arrest had given me. This was a week of bad news.

Just when I was most depressed, I came down with a new illness, which came on so quickly that I had to refocus on my own problems.

I had once had occasion to see, at Adolphe's, a young man who had a charming mistress named Angéline. Her face was delicate, as vivacious as possible. She had been registered as a prostitute when very young, and she had ended up in some horrible situation. Making virtue into a vice, she lived very modestly with her lover, who was ignorant of her position.

I would meet this young man again one day when I came to Lise's to try a new approach, since my usual attempts to hear news of her were no longer working.

"My dear Céleste," he said, grabbing hold of my arm to stop me, "it's so sad. A dozen of us were at a masked ball three days ago. We were having supper before going to l'Opera, and Angéline had on a charming outfit. You know how well she dances—everyone watches her, and they egg her on. She's a little too free-spirited, and a city sergeant told her that he was going to put her out. I came down to the foyer at that moment. My friend with whom she'd been dancing said there was a quarrel, and they were taken to the station. We were outraged. We wanted to fight them, but they held onto the poor girl. When she'd recovered her composure, they told her that she could be taken to jail. She didn't beg, she only asked permission to go up to her place, saying that she couldn't present herself before the magistrate in an undershirt. They accompanied her to the coach. At her building, she asked the police to wait five minutes while she took the time to write a note to her mother and me. The men impatiently tapped their toes outside her door. 'Come in!' she said. When they opened the door, they saw her disappear through the window, then they heard the body hit the pavement. They found two letters, and they sent this one to me."

He read the letter through tears:

My poor friend, I am going to take a difficult leap at my age. I'm not yet twenty. It isn't life that I'll miss, it's you. It's not death that I fear, it's maiming myself without dying because then you wouldn't love me anymore. Have me buried. If my head is not disfigured, kiss me.

I am a registered prostitute. In the two years that I've been with you, I've hidden this from you. I was so afraid you'd scorn me! I'm removing myself from registration. I was taken in yesterday, and I would pay for it for the rest of my days.

I would like my body to be taken to Saint-Lazare. You'll pity me; you'll look down on me. Don't miss me more than I am worth, but don't forget me too quickly. Adieu!

"She killed herself!" I said, touched to my soul.

"No, she broke both legs. She'll be crippled all her life, but I will take care of her. I'll never leave her."

I wanted to hug him, but I gave him a firm handshake and said, "You are a strong man. Kiss her for me."

He walked away. I looked around in fear. I was in the

same position she was.

I had thought Angéline was happy—happier than me. It was impossible that she wouldn't have scars, and would probably end up with as many as I did.

I didn't have any hope of waiting around very long for the object of my desires, because the curse of my fame would create double the obstacles. I couldn't resign myself to returning to the police station, where those women cling to looking like they're fifteen under threat of punishment. I lived outside the law: they would have the right to arrest me no matter where they found me. Realizing this, I could only shiver as I walked. I never crossed the boulevards; the Montmartre quarter was full of registered women, so surveillance was more active there. Each time a man looked at me, I thought it was a policeman. I ran as fast as I could, my heart racing.

This life, dominated as it was by fear, was awful. I didn't dare set foot into the night. Once, someone stole my watch. I had held onto it tightly; the day I got it, it was as if I possessed the treasures of Peru. But out of fear of having to state my name to the police, I didn't dare report the theft.

I thought I would be saved from that life by performing at Beaumarchais. I imagined that I was going to establish myself, to earn money. It was yet another illusion.

I was welcomed at Beaumarchais with open arms. They had me perform and dance all evening, but they didn't give me a regular slot. I asked if it would be like this for long, and I was told no, that the theater was about to close. This was a real bolt out of the blue. Misery, which I thought I'd escaped, was coming back to knock on my door with even more menace.

An accident pulled me off this rotten path. One day when I felt even more down than usual, idleness took my steps to a seller of toiletries I knew who lived at no. 16 rue de Temple, Madame Alphonse. The depression made me talkative; I told her all of my woes. There was a tall, skinny old man present, gray-haired, with bad eyes, a bent nose, glasses, and diamonds on his fingers. He was well-dressed and energetic. It turned out that he owned the building. This gentleman seemed to listen with interest and looked at me so attentively that I had to wonder why, but I couldn't figure it out.

"I believe, mademoiselle," he said after much consideration, "that I can offer you more advantageous employment than what you lost at Beaumarchais. I'm looking for trick riders for the Hippodrome. It needs young, elegant women."

"Here is your opportunity!" Madame Alphonse said to me.

"You have skill and courage; you can quickly learn to ride a horse. We're going to open a magnificent Hippodrome on the place de l'Étoile. You will be well paid."

I asked how much.

"That depends on your abilities and what you know. For now, I can give you one hundred francs a month, and I will teach you myself."

"That's very tempting," I said. "You'll put it in writing?"

"Immediately, if you like."

"I would prefer the theater, but to earn a hundred francs a month? I'll consider it. First of all, let me tell you that I'll work so hard that you'll be forced to give me a raise next year." I paused. "Well! I've considered. It's done. When is my first lesson?"

"Next week, if you want. Tomorrow I'll introduce you to my son." He took care to get my address then left.

When he'd gone, Madame Alphonse said to me, "You certainly know how the ball bounces. You'll learn one thing from this, anyway: how to ride a horse, and from the premier master of riding in Paris. There's no man as remarkable as M. Laurent Franconi. No one could replace him. He'll do for you in a month what others couldn't do for you in a year."

All was arranged and signed the next day. My stint ended at Beaumarchais, and I left the theater.

They say that bad luck never arrives alone. I believe that the same goes for good luck.

I felt joyful. I ran to Lise's house with a happy hunch. I wasn't wrong—she had returned. They'd released her the night before.

She was so ashamed that she didn't want to see anyone. I didn't think this applied to me, so I went up to the second floor. She was in a small room on the courtyard. The key was in the door, so I went in without knocking. I found her stretched out on a little sofa of painted wood, her arms along her sides, her face taut, her eyes ringed with black circles. Her lungs rattled so much that she wasn't breathing. I took her hand; it was cold.

"Lise," I said sweetly.

She opened her eyes and looked at me without seeing me. "Who is there?"

"It's me. I'm sorry to wake you, but your sleep seemed disturbed."

"My dear Céleste. I know that you've come by many

times. I wanted to go to your place, but I didn't have the courage. I am broken. You don't think I stole anything, do you?" she said with wild eyes as she clutched my arms.

"Non, that's why I'm here. But tell me what happened, because it sounds like a dream."

"A bad dream," she said.

Lise's Version

You know how I was arrested. They went through my papers and didn't find anything that could make anyone believe that I was an accomplice of these men. For a while, they argued that the shipments of money by post hadn't arrived. They complained, they searched, but it was impossible to discover who was responsible. After about three months, a young man showed up at the post office to pick up an order. At the same time, a gentleman who was waiting for his money had come to make a complaint. This second gentleman heard his name being called and was surprised to see the first young man sign for and hold in his hand the letter that he himself had not received. They went to stop the young man and searched him. He had several unsealed letters on him, each with a different address. At first, he didn't want to answer any questions or say who he was, but in the end he admitted everything.

It was a huge crime ring. There were seven or eight people in it, and they had an inside man at the post office. Every time a letter came in with money inside, this employee took it, then his accomplices came and picked it up. If it turned out the letters contained anything they couldn't steal, they burned them.

You've figured out who the employee at the post office was, so you understand the judge's suspicion. They thought I was an accomplice! If he'd forgotten a stolen letter at my house, even if I had no knowledge of it, I would have been done for!

He defended me, he showed up as much as he could. The magistrate who interrogated me said, "It seems he did it all for you."

I answered, "That's possible. I'm just that unlucky. But I don't doubt my own actions at all." Having innocence and truth on your side gives you strength.

The trial dates were approaching, and they saw that long before he knew me, he had done these same kinds of thefts. It was a sorry business. His father is one of the most important people in Toulouse and of the highest rank. They recognized my innocence and let me go, but I'm no less done for. Where could I go? I no longer dare show myself!

"No need to be discouraged," I said. "You're not guilty. Stay home for a while, don't go out. This will all be forgotten."

She shook her head in disbelief. "And you," she said, "what are you up to?"

"I left the theater and am working at the Hippodrome."

"I would love to ride a horse."

"Do you want to work at the Hippodrome with me? Nothing could be easier. I'll speak to M. Franconi."

She smiled sadly. "No, don't say anything."

There was a knock at the door. She hid behind the curtains and said, "I don't want to see anyone."

I opened the door. It was a tall, young blond man, so young he didn't even have to shave. He wasn't an attractive boy, but his face was pleasant enough.

"Could I see Lise?" he asked, almost in a whisper.

"Oh, it's you, Camille. Come in," said Lise before I could answer. She kissed him noisily on his cheeks. "Camille is not *anyone*," Lise said to me, laughing.

"Non," said the young man, "I'm not anyone, and I'm sorry, because if I were anyone, none of that would have happened."

"We'll take care of this later," she said, gripping his hand.

"I was scared," he said to her. "At last, you're free. I escaped; my tutor is waiting for me. I have to get back." And I heard him jump down the stairs four at a time, like a schoolboy.

"What is this young man?" I asked Lise.

"He's barely more than a child. He's nineteen, twelve years from reason. He invites himself up. For four months, he said to me every day, 'You see, Lise, I don't love you like everyone else does. Maybe if I begged, and you wanted, I could have you. But that's not what I want. I'll just be your friend, since I would suffer too much if I had to share you with others. When I'm an adult, I'll have a huge fortune. Then you'll be all mine. I'll take you away, and I'll make you so happy that you'll regret nothing that's ever happened in your life.'"

"Is it true that he'll inherit a fortune?" I asked. "Be careful around big talkers. This doesn't seem at all clear to me."

"There's no danger. He's the son of an immensely rich businessman. When his father died, he left him in the hands of a tutor who can only hand over his accounts when he's twenty-one."

"I see your future is secure. Very secure, I'd say."

"Do you think so?" she said as she got up. "He'll forget me before long, or I could very well die." She hit her chest, coughed, and said, "Do you hear that? I feel the phlegm."

"Come on! Where do you get these ideas? You'll live longer than me, and in my family, we go to a hundred years. I'm leaving. I'll come back to see you during the week."

I left feeling very joyful. Lise was free! And I had 120 francs from work.

13.

The Hippodrome

It wasn't enough to be called a horseback rider; I had to learn my job. Horseback riding and equestrian shows are no more improvised than any other performance.

I worked extremely hard. I took two or three lessons a day, along with an hour of dressage. In the beginning, I was very tired. I spit blood, but that didn't stop me.

I had to neglect many of my friends. Brididi was the one who suffered the most, because he'd developed a great affection for me. When I noticed he was getting a little too interested in me after our shared triumph at Mabille, I thought the best way to cure him of it was to take him into my confidence about the feelings I had for another. This turned out to be not at all the best way. First, M. Brididi was not as thoroughly discouraged as I thought he would be. Then, because I'd kept him up to date on my love life, he took advantage of my breaking up with Adolphe. When I started at the Hippodrome, Brididi was still very actively courting me.

A song had been written about Pomaré. It was attributed to a very clever man and based on the waltz of Rosita:

O Pomaré, my young and crazy queen,
Keep up the energy that surrounds you,
May the cancan always reign
And Chicard dim under your gaze!
Your flower-covered throne at Mabille
Holds all of our merry band.
Better to reign a hundred years there than on some island
Where our rainbow would stop sparkling.

Plus a hundred other verses I'm forgetting.

I had my own poets. Brididi sent me a letter in verse; unfortunately, he danced better than he sang. Now that I'm thinking about it, I realize that its rhythm is too off for me to reproduce it here. In these verses, M. Brididi spoke as all lovers speak. He reproached me for not loving him as much as he loved me, and he ended with a line that I promised him I found charming. He told me that I was for him what Lise was to Béranger.

My work at the Hippodrome took me far from the scene where I had met Brididi. I was like Lise, in that I was unfaithful to his friendship, but I always kept him in my memories.

At last the day came: my instructor was pleased with my riding ability. I would appear in three performances on opening day. The first was a parade that they called "the march." The second was a race, and the third a stag hunt. Those who attended the opening of the Hippodrome can still remember the spectacle.

I entered the area at the head of a column of four horses. I was dressed in a modest long-sleeved dress and apron like Jewish women wore, as were all the other riders. I heard my name going around: "Where is Mogador?" "Oh! There's Mogador!" They were talking so loudly I thought they were going to strangle me or shout something nasty.

There were more than eight thousand people crowded on top of one another. It was magnificent to see. All of elite Paris was there. These new costumes and this new venue had a marvelous effect. The sun sparkling on the sequins warmed their hearts, which had been a little cold toward us at first. The public applauded wildly at our entrance.

Two or three acts came before my next appearance. I was on my horse half an hour ahead of time. There were five of us in this act. I was shaking so badly I couldn't hold on to my horse. *I can no longer hold myself up,* I thought. *I'm going to fall!* And I tipped forward in the saddle.

I felt something lash my back, and I heard M. Laurent say to me, "Are you going to hold on like that? Straighten up, please."

I threw myself back.

"Good! Like a broom handle," he said. "Settle yourself in your saddle, body erect without being stiff, elbows against your sides, head forward. Grip with your fingers but not too hard…good! And don't be afraid. You have a good horse." He patted him on the neck.

As he walked past a gentleman, M. Laurent said, "It is what it is. That's my student. She's doing well, but she only had two months to learn." This compliment made me happy, but it didn't stop my heart from beating in my throat.

The curtain opened for my next act, the race. Out of fear that they'd say I was brazen, I lowered my eyes and squinted. We came to our marks, arranged ourselves in a line, and someone called out, "Go!"

My horse carried me like the wind, taking my breath away. I laid along his neck like jockeys do. I shouted at him, and he raced harder. I was going to pass my companions—maybe win the race! The thought transported me. I threw my horse over the rope in a turn, cutting across my closest competitor, and passed her! I was so happy yet so afraid that another would overtake me and win that I closed my eyes. I left it all to my horse, and I used my spur on his left flank.

I heard someone say, "She won!" Then the applause!

I gripped my knees harder against the horse. I took another lap. I was stopped and given a bouquet. I had won!

France was mine. I walked ahead of the others, and the audience applauded. My horse, who had raced hard, did a thousand leaps, which I rode gracefully enough. The bravos and compliments held me on my horse. I was radiant as I went backstage. My instructor shared in my joy.

Once I'd dismounted, my colleagues were looking for a fight. They said that I had narrowly missed spilling them off their horses, that I shouldn't have cut them off. I knew they were right, but I sent them packing.

I looked at my horse. He had a spot of blood on his side. I begged him for all the forgiveness in the world. I showed him my bouquet and gave him excuses, which I helped him to understand courtesy of a lot of sugar cubes.

I got dressed for the hunt. I had a splendid costume, and I was as happy as I'd ever been. I mounted a horse named Aboukir from the herd. I made him skip about as much as I could.

The stag was released. I took my role seriously, and I laughed with the lords who were placed in the center, waiting for the hunters and houndsmen to release the dogs.

This hunt was the kind of success the organizers of the show certainly had not dreamed of. When the dogs, who had been kept in kennels for days, were set free and put on the trail of the stag, they began running left and right, committing acts of indiscretion that ended up on both our horses and the hems of our dresses. The Parisian public, who saw everything and thought it all great fun, quickly noticed the mishap that was giving the houndsmen fits. They twisted themselves into knots with laughter.

Finally the stag was put on the right track, and the dogs saw him. The stag, already tired out by this point, retraced his steps to cross in front of the dogs. This was their whole reason for running! People clapped harder than ever.

I went out after the show, feeling more triumphant than a conquering general after a huge battle. I held my bouquet in my arms so everyone could see it.

Back at home, I asked my porter to put up the For Rent sign. I couldn't live here long. The next day, I found a small apartment, no. 1 fauborg Saint-Honoré, in the fifth arrondissement. There was a bedroom at the back and a kitchen. I was happy enough with it that I sublet the suite where I'd been living and moved house immediately. I left that quarter with pleasure. It seemed I could breathe easier in the new neighborhood. I arranged a little garden for myself on the drainpipe, which stuck out a foot and made a little shelf by the window.

The life I'd adopted put me into contact with a great number of women. Less out of preference than out of necessity, my life was like a kaleidoscope. I no longer saw Denise and Marie. They didn't lead lives any more moral than mine, but as courtesans they were thrown into other whirlwinds. Every day I had not new friends, but new relationships. I've composed many volumes with portraits and character sketches of the women who passed through my life, but I restrain myself as much as I can. I try to only get attached to those memories that seem interesting or that are necessary for telling my tale.

I knew, at the happiest moment of my life, a great woman who was neither brunette nor blonde, neither beautiful nor ugly, neither kind nor nasty. I gave her a piece of advice I'd always practiced. Believe me, I don't go looking for ways to fool myself. I know that fancy vice is still vice. But I always thought that, even when doing something wicked, there's an advantage in paying attention to the people in high society. The best people are wise, but even when they're not, it's better to be the mistress of a great lord than an upstart, or of a man of good taste than of a boor, or of a man of wit than a sot. I learned this subtlety, this ability, despite my moral downfall. I experience the pleasures of wit and the enjoyment of art, and find among the highest ranks of any society happy coincidences and lasting friendships, being a survivor of too easy love affairs.

The woman I gave this advice to profited by it. She met a Russian noble who, thinking her neck and arms too long, covered them in diamonds to hide her deformity. She ran into me again and, under the pretext that we were neighbors, had me up to her rooms. She spent the day showing me her riches, saying, "You would like this, eh?" and "If you could have this!" My heart was full, and I didn't know why.

She had a great passion for artists and spent her evenings in small theaters, giving herself entirely over in turn to a comic, a lover, a villain. She was only generous toward the arts. They said that she let a diamond fall from her bracelet at each of her favorite theaters.

She asked me to dine with her and go to a show that night. She told me that she was going to loan me a shawl in case I got cold. This touched me, and I said to myself, *This is definitely a woman of quality.*

I was very quickly disabused of that idea. She couldn't go to the theater alone; she needed a companion. She couldn't wear all her shawls at one time; she needed a mannequin.

Here's proof: She took me to dinner in a small restaurant on the boulevard du Temple. There were many actors who came in after us. We were served soup, and I was about to take a bite when, grabbing my arm, she said in her braying voice, "Be careful, you're going to stain my shawl!"

I turned crimson. It was solely for this reason that

she'd loaned the shawl to me. I'll leave you to wonder if my gratitude flew away.

That didn't stop her from pursuing me with offers of friendship. The maddest, most eccentric idea came to her in order to make this friendship seem somehow better in the eyes of the circles in which we moved: to pass me off as her sister. She begged me to say I was her sister because it would allow her more freedom. Then her Russian noble would allow her to go out with me.

In truth, she attached herself to me because I was Mogador. A nickname—as M. Véron noted with much finesse in *Memoires d'un Bourgeois de Paris*—a famous name for women like us is a fortune.

Some days after this, *my sister* asked me to accompany her to an artists' party. I was in the same position as before: I didn't have the necessary dresses. She generously put her entire wardrobe at my disposal. I refused, remembering, *Take care not to stain my shawl*. But it needed an arm to wear it no matter what it cost her.

To overcome my resistance, she used a little strategy that I had the good graces to let myself fall for. She bought me what I needed and said, "Here, this is all for you." I naturally thought that she was giving it to me: a set of flowery jewels worth five hundred francs, long gloves, a coach rented for the night—all things I'd never let myself spend money on. I thanked her for her generosity.

"Good! Good!" she said. "You can pay me back later."

A few days later, she sent me a one-hundred-franc invoice. I had never made anything like this much extra money. I had enough to live and pay my bills. I made her wait.

She became annoyed with me and created a scene in

front of everyone. I gave her the one hundred sous, or ten francs, that I had in my pocket.

One day not long after, I was at the theater in a box for six. She opened the door to my box and said at the top of her lungs, "Tell me, when are you going to pay me?"

I didn't have anything on me that day. One of the people I was with asked me how much I owed her and settled my debt.

At this moment, you understand, the split between us was complete.

She went around saying to everyone, "I am mad at *my sister*."

We remained quarreling for a long time, to her regret, because I began to make a lot of nasty noise.

&

I had learned new routines at the Hippodrome—and learned that there was one row of hedges that would cost me dearly. I rode a sweet chestnut mare that had incredible energy. She would shiver for an hour before showtime, and by the time they opened the gate, she was already dripping with sweat.

Once, she puffed herself up when she was being saddled, and they forgot to check her again before leaving the paddock. During the show, I felt myself slipping. I wanted to stop, but I was right in front of the hedge, and she jumped. I did my best to throw myself to one side so I wouldn't be dragged alongside her hooves, and I fell onto the trail beside the hedge. I was about to get up when I saw hooves over my head. All the horses and riders who followed me were jumping the hedge.

Those few seconds were awful for me—and for the audience. My foot got trampled; my mare had stomped on me as she fled. It wasn't fractured, and the injury was nothing. I asked for my horse to be brought around and I remounted in front of the audience. They had an endless affection for me and proved it by applauding with all their might.

This kind of show had the attraction of being novel. It was the loud enthusiasm of the crowd that gave us courage. They clapped so wildly it could be frightening. The audience often yelled, "Enough! It's too much!"

You couldn't hear a thing, and the luck we had was almost unbelievable. There were always accidents where someone should have died, but they survived with only bruises. I could have had my hand or ribs cracked that day at the hedge. I rested at home in my chair for a week, then I went back to work with more passion than ever.

The perils of performing were not the only ones I was exposed to at this time in my life. There was also a danger in the growing number of my fans.

As soon as a woman is well known in Paris, if she is not protected by an unassailably virtuous reputation, she's put on the rack. There are young women who, out of politeness or foolishness, believe that they have to respond to every advance. Those women will fall within a few months. Abandonment and scorn don't lessen the excitement. I was neither polite enough nor stupid enough to bring myself to that point. Lucky for me, I had quickly understood that gallantry is like war: to secure victory, you have to use tactics. Even in the early days, I had two faults that served me well in defending myself. I had always been mercurial and haughty. None of these women who were inclined to say yes got any more pleasure out of it than I did saying no. Besides, the men who have the most to get from you are the ones who ask the least.

The more a woman has a reputation for being easy to get along with, the more she needs to feed everyone's desire for her. I, however, needed to maintain my reserve due to my past.

Those who wanted to get into my good graces didn't always explain themselves to me using their own voices. Usually they appealed to me in a roundabout way by sending ambassadors to my apartment. In a single week, I received I don't know how many women who came to announce my admirers to me and do their best to negotiate alliances. I stopped them in their tracks. I didn't want to be associated with these women, for whom I had the deepest aversion, at any price. So they furiously descended my building's five flights of stairs. When they took stock of their mission, they couldn't believe it. They thought, I admit with a blush, that the conquest of Mogador would be easy.

I had to congratulate myself for the role that I played. People's opinion of me changed. They didn't stop seeking my attention, but they put it more delicately and gave me time to breathe and make choices.

Here again, I find a memory of *my sister*. Since I refused to see her, another idea came into her head: to send me a lover. A young, more-or-less-German baron who had an office at the court of … was among those government officials whom I turned away. He told *my sister* of his defeat.

"Introduce yourself and say I sent you," she said to him with her usual haughtiness. "You are sure to receive an excellent welcome."

He believed her and came to my house, convinced that he would present himself under the best auspices. This was a thirty-five-year-old man, blond, tall enough and handsome enough, with a kind and distinguished demeanor.

He too was let down. I was still the flower of his heart, but he comported himself like a man of intelligence. Picking up on my true feelings for my dear sister, he admitted that he couldn't stand her, and he told me so many terrible stories that I couldn't help but listen.

"Your turn now," he said.

I too had many nasty tales that needed to be aired. Our conversation went on. Gossip helped it along, and the baron received permission to visit again.

He took advantage of that invitation many times. He had a quick mind, which is the most irresistible kind of seduction. It's possible that I had once again, against my will, fallen under the indirect influence of my sister. But the baron was soon ordered to return to Holland.

After nursing my sore foot at home, I went back to work at the Hippodrome.

The young, fashionable people—or those who wished to be young and fashionable—came in through an entrance at the side of the stables, where each of us riders had our fans. There was one man who busied himself with a relentless obsession with me. He was a young, skinny, brown-haired man, very carefully groomed. He constantly looked at me with his large, beautiful black eyes. Although his eyes lacked any kind of spark, they expressed well enough what he wanted me to understand.

He never dared speak to me.

I asked one of my friends, "Who is this young man who follows me everywhere and seems himself to be injured every time I make a mistake?"

"My dear," answered Hermance, a pretty little Englishwoman who wore a wig, "he's the son of a pharmacist."

"That's too bad. He's nice."

"If you don't help him along a little," another woman said, "he'll never dare speak to you. He's very rich. His father is a big manufacturer of locomotives."

"A minute ago, he was a pharmacist. I should listen to you instead."

I mounted my horse and entered the arena.

My saddle was not tight enough, so I stopped in front of the box seating before the race began. While my horse's straps were tightened, I heard the muddled sound of praise—always music to a woman's ears. I forgot about my fall the last time I'd performed and promised myself that I'd earn this praise if I could. I urged my mare on, and I came in first by half a head.

When I returned to the stables, I saw that my fans were all ashen. Their eyes were shining as if they were full of tears. The young man came up to me and said, "You gave me a fright! I thought I was going to see you fall a dozen times."

I wanted to tell him that he was being far too kind.

It was impossible for me to untangle myself and leave at that moment. The ice had been broken. He followed me to the door of my dressing room, and I closed it in his face.

He came to see me at home the next day, which I had not given him permission to do. He wouldn't leave my house. He was a hay-eating idiot, but such a nice boy, so obliging, and above all so amorous that I was often tempted to give in to him despite my repugnance for stupid men.

His name was Léon. You understand, without my having to explain, that discretion prevents me from adding family names. There are secrets that not everyone needs to know. Let the curious look and the clever learn.

I was becoming a good rider.

❧

I asked the court for my freedom from the prostitution rolls once. They said that it hadn't been long enough since leaving the bordello. If the Hippodrome closed, they pointed out, I would still have to make a living somehow. I went home discouraged and in tears. Women were still bringing me more brilliant propositions than I'd ever received before. I thought that these women had been sent by the police, and I received each of them more rudely than the one before.

One evening I went to Ranelagh with one of my colleagues from the Hippodrome, Angèle. We sat in the corner of the room and chatted. A flower seller came over with magnificent roses for me.

"On behalf of those gentlemen," she said, pointing to two men seated some way from us. Both were short, one blond with an unremarkable face and a common look, as if his foot wasn't as long as my hand. The other was a nice-looking boy, younger and cheeky as a pageboy.

I wanted to refuse the flowers to irritate them.

"Are you nuts?" said Angèle. "Keep them. Can't you see that they're lovely?"

I didn't say anything. I set the flowers on a chair in front of me without looking at the men who sent them.

They came over. The younger of the two took the lead and said to me, "You don't like the flowers! I am sorry to offer you something so ugly. If you'll let me, I'll bring you others."

I responded with a small nod and a little pout, as if to say, *Thank you for the first bouquet, but I will not take any more.*

"I see, mademoiselle, that you don't like small talk. This is evidence of intelligence." He moved in closer and set his chair on the hem of my dress. I pointed this out to him and made him back off. "Non," he said, "I've already damaged it. I'll send you a new one."

His friend, who had remained standing, said something to him in another language. He answered in the same language and turned back to me.

"The duke is right. I don't have the right to flirt with you. The duke and I, we've seen you on your horse, and we've both fallen in love. We flipped a coin, and the winner has the right to climb the ladder into your good graces. I lost. The duke sent one of his friends to your apartment, and you met him at your door. Thinking that the duke had given up all hope, I did the same thing he had done. My man's reception was no better."

"And this surprises you?"

"Oui. We bet fifty louis." He told me this so presumptuously that I seized on immediate revenge.

"I assure you, monsieur," I said, "there is no game more innocent than that. Since you anted up, you would need to be assured of my consent, and that's a condition that your bet will never get you. I promise you that if I had to make a choice between you two, I would choose to leave." I didn't imagine that, in being so rude, I was making an impression on his friend.

The friend noticed and wanted me to know that he liked me very much. Being polite yet serious and self-possessed, he was the complete opposite of the other. Maybe he'd been stifled by the difficulty of the language, because he spoke French with a southern accent. But I had raised my head to look at him, and to irritate his friend, I made small talk.

The duke asked permission to come see me. I granted it, saying loudly, "It would give me great pleasure."

This worked, because the shorter gentleman left his seat, saying, "That's what it means to be a duke worth 300,000 francs." His snit did him no good. This enumeration of his rival's advantages was not at all a good way to inspire me to dislike my new admirer. It's part of the world I lived in: a title and thousands of francs don't exactly keep you out of a woman's heart.

Once we were alone, the duke became more talkative. It was up to him to continue the conversation. "What a funny character is my friend! He is a charming boy, but he is a little conceited. Everyone has to give in to him. He has, otherwise, a lot of success with women. He thinks that when they prefer me, it is for my wealth. That makes me suspicious of them, and I end up believing it."

The provocation was direct, and while I had never liked a man fishing for compliments, I resigned myself to be gracious enough to say to the duke that he was wrong about himself.

He offered his arm for a walk about the garden. I accepted with double pleasure: first because it flattered my vanity, and second because it was a way to continue to bother his friend, toward whom I wanted to be so brutal.

I had always detested men who put on airs of authority over me.

In retracing these memories of my life, I experience a particular effect: I am happiest when sharing my mistakes, though in my youth I never thought about them while committing them. Decency and studiousness are required, and between them there is a mysterious rapport that reveals my slumbering conscience. At every turn, I've been tempted to conceal the unavoidable reality, but I haven't given in to the temptation. I understand that my tale would lose all interest if I stopped being sincere.

My liaison with the duke put me in an entirely new position. It granted me entry into the wider world of bohemia. I rose too high not to have enemies. Nothing got by me, not even the jealousy of my friends, who shredded me with their sharp teeth.

The duke was not at odds with his friend. We saw him often. He'd lost neither his cool nor his hopes. "You'll come back to me," he told me. "It's only a matter of time. The duke can't keep you forever."

"Never," I answered. I kept my word.

He consoled himself with Angèle.

12.

Lise's Yellow Dress

As soon as anything, good or bad, happened to me, my first thought was to go to see Lise, to share my joys and sorrows with her. She had told me about her plan to take a short trip, but she would be back. Her landlady, who knew of our close friendship, gave me her new address under seal of secrecy, because Lise persisted in not wanting to see anyone. She was living at no. 107 Champs-Elysées, in the fifth arrondissement. I knocked on her door there.

"Come in!" said a well-known voice.

I opened the door, and I saw my Lise stretched out on her bed, a candle lit for her cigarette, a book in her hand.

"Oh, it's you! You're kind to come see me, but if the other one comes back, she's going to throw a fit. She can't stand you."

I looked around the room. It was a cozy space and respectable enough. "Whose place is this?" I stood up to go.

She grabbed onto my dress. "That's right, you don't know. Stay a minute! She won't eat me alive."

Eulalie

Remember after my arrest when I didn't dare go out? I didn't want to stay in that building any longer. I was in the middle of feeling sorry for myself when a young woman said she wanted to speak to me—no matter what. I thought it was a ruse, that it was some creditor. I told off my landlady, who went downstairs to deliver that same telling off to the young lady.

After a few seconds, my landlady came back up and said, "This young lady insists. She says that when I tell you her name, you'll see her."

If I had been standing, I would have fallen flat out. It was my sister Eulalie! What did she want with me? I immediately assumed that my father was downstairs waiting to strangle me.

I told the landlady, "Close the doors. I'm not here. My God! It's all over! Say that I don't know her, that she's mistaken."

"But I'm not mistaken," said Eulalie, sticking her head through the doorway.

I ran around behind her and shut the door, throwing my body against it with all my might.

"Oh my, what are you doing?" she said, laughing.

I looked at her, and once I'd overcome my terror, I was struck by her elegant dress. I listened at the door and heard nothing.

"What do you want from me? Our father is right

behind you, isn't he? Why did you bring him along, you backbiting shrew?"

"My God, you are stupid. He doesn't know where I am. He can't follow me here."

"How is it possible, mademoiselle, that our father doesn't know where you are? Unless you've run away from his house!"

"Oui. After you left, everything went from bad to worse. When Maxime left home, he brought me along to Paris. Since he didn't have much, I went to work at the Hippodrome. I earned a little money, which helped. Now I live at no. 107 Champs-Elysées. If you want to come with me, I can offer you half of my room."

Can you believe it? It was terrible to see my sister fallen so low. I went to apologize, but she stopped me.

"Don't make a fuss," she said. "It's not your fault I left home. I would have left anyway. I'm in love with Maxime."

I was stunned, but I didn't have any right to scorn her. Besides, it would have been perfectly useless. You can only imagine how embarrassed I was for how I had behaved.

I had a pretty large debt at my building and no money to pay it off. I moved to her room with two chemises, a pair of slippers, and the dress I had on. I said that I was leaving for the country, but I went nowhere, really.

But I have to leave this situation. I've been a weight on my sister. She had offered her home to me, as almost anyone would, but also as almost anyone would, she regretted it. First off, she's not rich, and she knows that this arrangement doesn't put me in the best position. She's stingy. Yesterday she yelled at me for buying a packet of cigarette papers. We fight twenty times a day.

After each scene, I put my two chemises in my trunk. Eulalie can't help but laugh, and I stay, promising to pay her, which I know isn't going to happen. I had to accept that she was right.

Look at this little room—it's so tidy because there's almost nothing in it. But it's nice and all. She follows me all day with a towel to clean up my footprints. I stay in my bed. That way I don't mess anything up.

I couldn't help but laugh, because the bed, the nightstand—the whole room—looked as if it had been pillaged, even the books, and the torn cigarette papers thrown here and there, the tobacco, the ashes….

"I'll get out of here," I said, standing. "She's not always friendly, your Eulalie. I often saw her at the Hippodrome without knowing she was your sister, and I've already had two or three run-ins with her. If she finds me here, she's capable of saying something awful."

"Non, stay! Stay a little longer. She won't be back for at least an hour. She's at Maxime's, and I know how to put her in a good mood." She began straightening up around herself and wiping the table with her only dress. "Now, open the window to let all the smoke out."

"At least you have a good view to distract you."

"That doesn't distract me at all. It makes me desperate to make a break for it. I bore myself to tears."

I went back to sit near the bed. I was a little embarrassed by the proposition I wanted to make, because I knew how she was.

"Look, my dear Lise, if you're bored with yourself here, would you like to leave? I'll get things ready for you as much as I can. If you want to move to my place, I'm at your service. I'm not your sister. I won't make a scene."

"Non," she said, "I still love having a friend more than having money. If I owed you money, that would may be the end of us—not because of you. I know that you'd never blame me at all. But I would be humiliated. I know myself; I don't need a lot. Look, my eyebrows come together like a pair of little mustaches. They say it's a sign of jealousy. I'm afraid the saying might be true. The jealousy would be stronger than me. I love you very much, but I couldn't live with you. If you were doing better than me, then your good luck would end up making me sad." She had tears in her eyes as she spoke.

I took her hand. "I'm glad you're being straight with me. Nothing would be worse for me than being angry with you. Wait! Someone's coming up. If it's Eulalie—"

We didn't have to wait long to find out if it was. The door opened, and Eulalie seemed very surprised to see me there. Pomaré completely lost her composure. I was even more surprised because I knew few women whose personalities could dominate Pomaré. Her sister must have held a lot of sway over her. Eulalie was a medium-sized woman, plump, with a plain face and a very cold demeanor. Some thought she seemed stupid, but she had infinite intelligence. Where she was completely lacking, in my opinion, was in the fact that at seventeen years old she already looked twenty-five.

She waited for one of us to explain ourselves.

I had to break the silence. "You are surprised, my dear colleague, to find me paying you a visit, since you haven't spoken to me before. But I've just come from the Hippodrome. As I passed, I saw Lise at the window, and I came up."

She looked at me without saying hello and said to

her sister, "I told you not to open my window."

Color climbed up my face. *My little Eulalie,* I thought, *here's an arrogance that you can carry to hell.*

Lise sat dumbfounded at her air of authority. Luckily, I had a way to avenge both Lise's injuries and mine. I became the calmest person in the world.

"Even if I hadn't seen Lise, I would have come up anyway. I have a favor to ask of you."

"Of me?"

"Oui. I've often heard you feeling sorry for yourself because they don't put you in the races. They forget you among the extras."

She turned purple. I'd touched a sensitive nerve.

"Well, if you get the chance to show yourself in a steeplechase, I'm sure that they'll let you race in place of Hermance, who rides a horse like a hen."

"I'm perfectly aware," she said, "but they don't want to let me try."

"That's shocking. When they don't let you try, just say to the guys, 'You don't even know how to do my job.' I'm offering you a way to get into the good graces of the stage managers. I'm leaving in a few days, and I'd like one of my colleagues to take my role for two weeks. This is what I came to ask you, since I've just put in my request for vacation."

She was radiant with joy. I think she wanted to hug me.

"I'd like that very much," she said. "I'll show them that I'm good at something. Make sure they agree to it."

"I have a way to make them do it. I'm not going to tell them in advance. One day I won't be there, but you'll be ready, and they won't have a choice. They'll see that they were wrong about you."

"I must go back to Maxime's," she said. "He wasn't there a bit ago. Stay with Lise; I won't be long. If you can't stay, come back tomorrow. We'll talk."

Lise squeezed my hands. She understood. When Eulalie had gone, she said, "You know that it was nearly impossible for me to not burst out laughing in front of her. You told me an hour ago that she rode a horse as if she were jug of water!"

"My dear, that was the only way to see you. Nothing can be done about it. If I proposed it at the Hippodrome, they'd snort-laugh at me. And then there's another problem: I'm not actually leaving town. The idea is that in ten days, you won't live here anymore. Goodbye. Keep up this ruse, and I'll be back tomorrow."

Back at home, I wrote a note to the hotel des Princes, to a young man named Manby with whom I'd sometimes spent the evening at Lise's. He had assured her, in front of me, of his enduring friendship. He did not waste any time; at four o'clock, he was at my place.

"It's kind of you to come, my dear friend," I said. "I have a favor to ask of you."

"Anything you like, as long as you let me kiss you."

"You don't think that's what I'm going to ask for?"

"I didn't think of that. Sorry."

"All right, enough nonsense. Lise is miserable. She doesn't want to take anything from me, but from you she'll accept anything. She must leave her sister's place. Eulalie treats Lise like a dog."

"My dear," he said, "I hand my money over to you. I have only ten louis on me; here they are. If that's not enough, as long as she asks me in that same sweet voice, I'm always ready."

"She won't ask you for anything. She doesn't even

know that I wrote you. Goodbye, and thank you—for her."

The next day, I ran happily to Lise's. I said to myself, *She's going to rent herself a room and give a hundred francs to her landlady. Then she can leave behind her shame.*

I told her what I had done. She seemed pleased.

"Let's go do some shopping," she said. "I have a lot of little things to buy."

I wanted to say to her, "Slow down!"

We stopped at Bayadères on the boulevard. I waited for her in the carriage, and she came out an hour later with a package.

"Look at the pretty color!" She showed me a maize-colored taffeta. Gorgeous.

"What is that, exactly?"

"That? It's a dress."

"Yes, but how much did it cost?"

"One hundred sixty francs."

I thought her mad. I resolved to no longer go out of my way for her. I slumped down in the carriage.

Our coach did not move quickly. We'd rented it for an hour, and it glided along slowly. I was going to fauborg Saint-Honoré, she to the Champs-Elysées.

"Are you going to go away angry," Lise said, "because I bought myself a dress? This was too expensive for me. I know perfectly well that I should spend my money more wisely, but I want to go to Ranelagh on Thursday. I'm going to have the dress and matching capelet, and a beaded hat. They'll think I've made a fortune. They'll come over to talk to me. If I don't wear something breathtaking, they won't even ask me to dance for them."

One the one hand, I knew she was right. But I couldn't excuse this insanity. At that time, when I found myself ahead by twenty francs, I'd buy ten meters of calico at twelve sous to make chemises.

"Come on, let's make up," she said as she departed. "Give me your hand and promise to come get me Thursday at eight. I can't go out with my toilette, not in the day and not on foot."

"You're trying to say that I have to find a carriage for you. Fine! We'll go, but don't make this a habit."

I went down my street. I was about to climb my five flights of stairs when the porter knocked on his windowpane. He was a tailor with a room was at the end of the hall. He waved to me and held up a parcel. I ran, intrigued.

"There's something new," he said. "It smells good." He gave me a huge bouquet of the rarest flowers. "It came from people who asked for you. Then someone came from the commissioner's."

I hid my face in the bouquet as if breathing the flowers in, but I smelled nothing. I became very pale. I had to lean on the tailor's workbench.

He raised his glasses and said to his wife, "What did he say, the inspector?"

She left her place at the stove. She was a good woman, large, not wasting away. I often saw her at her door. "He said that if you haven't taken down the flowers over your window by tomorrow, you'll be fined."

I inhaled the emptiness of the tailor's room and climbed the stairs like a bird. I didn't want anything to do with the inspector. I opened my window and looked at my poor flowers that were climbing so enthusiastically.

"Dear sweet peas, nasturtium, and morning glory, I watered you, tended you with so much care. Must I destroy you? Little flowers for the poor, how I love you!" I set my beautiful bouquet aside. It seemed gaudy, so I tossed it into the bedroom, and I kissed my reseda and my pansies. I looked for a way to take them down without destroying them. I had made the planter myself and filled it with dirt. The vines and stems were enlaced in the iron grille work, impossible to untangle.

The ring of the bell made me jump. I threw myself at my garden and furiously ripped everything out. I heard the stems cry out. They seemed to reproach me for the death of my flowers. But I redoubled my efforts to remove the strings tying them up, which cut my fingers.

"They'll ask me why you aren't down. You can see that I had to pull you out!" I pushed my hands into the dirt.

The bell rang louder. I went to open the door.

It was Léon. The duke had forbidden my seeing him, but it was less out of affection for me than stubbornness.

"What the hell are you doing? I've been ringing for two hours!"

"Why were you ringing me?"

"Once you climb all the way up to your door, you don't want to have to go back down five flights of stairs."

"Who asked you to come up? You gave me a terrible fright."

"If you're busy, I'll go." Without waiting for my answer, instead of heading for the door, he went to the window. He picked up my bouquet. "I see you're ripping out your garden. It's no longer dignified enough for you, so everything around you must suffer the same fate. Your duke sent you these?" He tossed the bouquet back into the bedroom.

This irritated me. I picked up my bouquet, as it represented a person. I always defended those who weren't there to defend themselves. "I told you that I wanted to be free, that I would not be engaged to anyone. You said you loved me very much. The only way to prove it, the only way to keep my friendship if not my love, is to not tyrannize me."

"You're begging, Céleste. You call me a tyrant because I'm jealous. That's the best proof I can give you of my love. Hermance asked me to go see her. She would be thrilled if I said to her a quarter of what I came to say to you."

"Fine! Go say it all to her. I don't want to keep you."

Quarrels with Léon were plays in three acts. He began by being disrespectful, then he became smug, and he ended up by giving in. Only then would I soften my stance. This was the turn toward being smug.

He put a look of satisfaction on his face. He examined his trousers—purchased in London—his tasteful vest, his impeccably cut riding coat. It was as if he was saying to me, *How can you be disdainful of a man as well dressed and respectable as me?*

I knew women who were taken in by these fashionable creatures. I was not one of them. A man's pretentions and affectations always revolted me. I maintained a glacial silence. Poor Léon no longer knew where he stood. His impudence and his pride dropped to the floor.

As we talked, I took down the stalks and cut the strings holding up my plants—not without sorrow and regret.

"Why are you so hard on yourself by taking down these flowers?"

"Because I was told to take them down."

"By who?"

"The commissioner." Léon looked at me so sadly and apologetically that I was disarmed. I held his hand.

"Look, I know I was short with you. I'm sorry. You know very well that I'm blunt and bad-tempered, but it passes quickly. It's because of my garden. I have my reasons for not wanting to be fined over it."

"You don't have money? There's no reason for that to be a problem. I'd gladly be your banker." Better to let him think of it this way than to not let him think of it at all.

I told him I was going to Ranelagh then next day. He said he would send a carriage for me.

⁂

I looked for Lise at the appointed hour. She was gorgeous, and we took two or three laps in the carriage before going to the ball. On the way, she told me that little Camille had come to see her, and that it was the same as always.

"I'm glad," I said. "I believe in him, myself."

"It's most extraordinary; he never changes. He always says, 'I wouldn't give up on making you mine for anything in the world.' I did my best one time to make him lie, and he got out of it like Joseph. Poor schoolboy! He skimps on quills to send me flowers."

"Do your best to keep it going. I think men like him are rare—men who don't love you only out of love for themselves."

"Speaking of which, and of you, what is going on with Léon? They say he adores you and is very nice."

"Oui."

"Why didn't he come along with you?"

"Because I don't want him to anymore. The other day, at eleven, I was headed for the Hippodrome, and he offered to take me. I mentioned to him that everyone would see us in the carriage, that it would reflect poorly on his family. He scoffed and told me he wasn't at all afraid. We got to the top of rue de Chaillot, and he started to run like a thief being chased. Some people looked at me. I waited a few minutes. They stopped and asked me what was going on. Since I was embarrassed, I escaped out of my side of the coach. When I got back to my place, I found him at my door, hands in pockets and sniffling.

"'There you are,' I said. 'Are you going to tell me what kind of fly stung you?'

"'My dear, I saw we were about to pass my mother and grandfather. That would have been great if they'd seen Mogador on my arm!'

"'You're right, but then why offer to take me? I didn't ask you. In fact, it was just the opposite. To make sure that never happens again, we'll never go out together.'

"It's true that he has asked me since then, but I don't want to make a habit of not keeping my word. I won't give in."

Lise and I made a magnificent entrance at Ranelagh. I didn't have a yellow dress, but I had such a narrow waist that everyone remarked on it. I often chastise myself for this, because Lise wrapped her arms around herself as if she were in great pain.

The party burst into laughter. They got used to us. The proper ladies looked at us without too much wrath. The young family scions kept their heads and did not extend invitations to us. They didn't want to dance the quadrille and refused to partner with us, fearing, they said, to become part of a show like M. Brididi had. They stayed far away.

But they were on their own. The rest of the crowd surrounded us and laughed, the energy grew. The young men stopped dancing under the pretext that the shrieking kept them from hearing the beat. They ended up arguing about it being their turn to dance with us. But in trying to dance better than Brididi, they only made themselves look ridiculous.

A grand supper was arranged. Many carriages left in a train, and we arrived like a wedding party at café Anglais, which shook with our laughter all night, with our shrieks and our songs.

Pomaré often looked at me with a kind of envy.

I had a lovely voice and the charm of youth. I was given compliments that were hard for her to hear. I knew her nature, and I downplayed my friendships a little, which I would not at all do for any other woman.

There was a young man at this supper named Gustave. I noticed that he seemed preoccupied.

"What are you thinking about?" his friends asked him.

"I'm thinking of poor Alphonse, who's bored by the things that amuse us. Too bad he isn't here! This is what he needs to distract him. It's so sad to see such a charming boy let himself wither away. Boredom will kill him; he's done for."

"Who is this Alphonse?" I asked.

"He's a man of talent."

"Is he ill?"

"No, he's depressed."

"That's twice as bad. He must be distracted from it."

"You'll have to make an assault on him."

"That's an idea. I'll do my best. You're so cheerful and charming. If you'd like to take on this cure with me, I'm sure it'll succeed."

※

The next day, we received an invitation from M. Alphonse R…. They'd put it into his head to have some friends over. He gave a tea just to see us since they had spoken of so highly of our vivacity.

We arrived with Lise at nine in the evening, rue de Bruyère. We were led into a lovely apartment. I don't know what was going on with me that day; I was horribly depressed. This inspired Lise. We had the idea of wearing matching dresses, and we looked like mourners. And then to go the home of man who was dying! We wore sincere faces for the occasion.

The master of the house was tall and thin, and his cheeks were drawn and spotted. His face was sweet and refined, with a distinguished air and a rare friendliness. He greeted us, and we thanked him for sacrificing an evening to his shadow side. We were seated, and he himself offered us fruits, cake, and tea. Then, seating himself in an armchair, he stayed without moving, without seeming even to think.

I leaned toward Lise's ear and said, "I'm sorry to have come. I feel like I'm actually grieving."

His friend Gustave sat near him. His own mother couldn't have been more attentive. Clouds of concern passed over Gustave's face. "Alphonse, what are you thinking? You forget that we promised to be fun. The time has come for Pomaré to sing."

His intentions were admirable, but he spoke too loudly. Lise heard him, and finding herself being so rudely used in this way, she furrowed her brow.

M. Gustave came over to her, smiling as if he were

the last of his kind. "Would you, mademoiselle, be so kind as to sing something for us?"

"Non," said Lise drily. "I'm much less fun than you think."

M. Alphonse R… came over to join his friend so graciously that it seemed in poor taste to be so petty.

"You can't refuse now," I said to Lise.

"Is this request for you?" she said to Alphonse, who was approaching the piano bench.

It was, so she sang with spirit and incredible verve. Alphonse opened his eyes and ears: this seemed to entertain him very much. Gustave made a thousand kind gestures in Lise's direction for having come to make his dear friend smile. Lise, who was as mercurial as the moon, had completely forgotten her sullenness, and she and Gustave were now best friends.

That evening showed me a world that I hadn't known before. An easy gaiety reigned there, which was nicer than the exuberant joy that I was used to. The mind itself could be fun.

Someone began playing music. A short young man sat at the piano. From the first notes, I recognized a master. I watched him intently. He had curly blond hair, blue eyes, full lips, and white teeth. He was more handsome than not, but his face lacked expression. His hands ran over the keyboard lightly, with incredible agility. This wasn't music but a harmony that wrapped around your heart.

When he'd finished playing, unanimous and well-deserved applause filled the salon. I used the cover of the noise to ask M. Gustave who this young man with such talent was.

"Don't you know anyone at all, my dear child? That's H… the composer, H… the prodigy! I'll introduce you to him."

Without asking if I'd like that or not, he took my hand and led me to him. I thought I saw M. H... redden as he approached me.

"I am most grateful to my friend," he said to me with a trace of a German accent that was not at all disagreeable, "for steering me toward you. Since the first day I saw you, already quite some time ago, I wanted to meet you. The evening was getting late, and I was afraid I would miss my chance."

I asked him with a little trepidation where he knew me from.

"But I saw you riding a horse, and you carried away my heart, which has run with you ever since." He nodded and moved away.

M. Gustave, who'd stood nearby, said quietly, "He has a lot of talent, but he won't get very far if his parents, who are Israelites, don't make him use that talent. At eight years old, he was a remarkable force. He played concerts, he was all anyone talked about."

"What? He's Jewish?" I said with a little disdain that I admit I could not suppress.

I know this isn't discussed and that I seem to have fewer prejudices that other people, but at the time I was horrified by Jews. Here's where it came from: there were a lot of Jews in the quarter where we lived when I was a girl. My mother had always felt sorry for them. When we moved to rue du Temple, there was a Jewish family on the first floor. I often went to play with their two children. On their Sunday, which was Saturday, they couldn't touch money or do anything. They would ask me over to light their fire and do their shopping. Then their oldest daughter died on a Friday. I came on Saturday, as

I usually did, and I heard people talking. I looked though the glass windowpanes of the door, and I saw the young girl, dead and naked as a worm. Her mother washed her face, her chest; her little sister washed her feet. I didn't understand the customs of this religion, and it scared me. Torturing the dead seemed awful to me. After that, I didn't want to go into their apartment, and I couldn't shake that dark memory.

Poor H… made heroic efforts to attract my attention. He left the piano and came over to me. Not knowing what to say, he invited everyone to come spend the rest of the evening at his house on rue de Provence. Everyone else accepted. He awaited my response. To tease him, I said thank you, but I couldn't. I was busy.

"Let us do it another day," he said so loudly and quickly that I regretted my snarky refusal.

"No, I'll cancel my dinner and come to your place."

He took my hand and said in a beseeching voice, "Do not miss it. You would be doing me such a favor!" He squeezed my hand, which gave me chills. I had been awful! He was only a child at the time, and it was at this moment that he fell in love with me.

M. Alphonse wanted to have us over again as soon as the next day. Lise amused him very much. She seemed to have found a remedy for his depression. Gustave was delighted.

H… came along to see me home with the others. At my door, he took my hand and placed it on his heart. "Wait. See how I love you—my heart beats as if to bruise my breast. Worse, it is afraid of never seeing you again."

I took back my hand with a laugh and said, "How easily you catch fire! Come on, I'll spend the evening at your place to see if this fire always burns."

∞

Léon came to see me the next day. He was ashen.

"What's wrong?" I asked.

"It's nothing," he said seriously. "I have something I need to tell you."

"You know very well that I don't like secrets. Tell me what you came for."

"I had a fight yesterday at Tortoni. I duel tomorrow."

"You!" I said skeptically. "And why are you dueling?"

"Because…because…yesterday they spoke of you… in terms that disgusted me. I called one of these gentlemen a coward after he had thrown a five-hundred-franc bill on the table and said, 'That's the key to Mogador's heart.' I said he was lying, that his money had taken the place of his brains."

"My poor friend, I don't want you to duel, especially over me. He's not wrong. I should have told you what I was—a courtesan. I promise I won't leave people in the dark about it anymore. If I'd told you, you wouldn't have reason to take such offense. Léon, I beg of you, try to get out of this dueling business. If you come to harm because of me, I'll never forgive myself."

I fell prey to a horrible depression. We spent three hours crying. He told me that he would go arrange his affairs and see his mother. I didn't want to let him leave, but he was so resolute, and he seemed so calm, that I didn't dare say a word.

"Goodbye," he said as he kissed my hand. "If I'm not here at eight o'clock tomorrow morning, then it's all over for me. I can't always express my thoughts, but I love you more than I know how to say." He pulled open the door, and I heard him run like the wind down the stairs. I threw myself onto the bed and dissolved into tears.

"How unlucky I am! Woe is me, and woe to those who love me. Léon, poor thing! They're going to kill you!"

Duel for me! Is that possible? I didn't beg enough for him to stay. I am a horrible woman. I treat him so badly, and he's so good! I'm unfair! Ungrateful! If he returns, I'll gladly take him back. I'll ask his forgiveness. What's going to happen to him? I can't stay here. Each minute is a century.

I put on my hat and walked through quarter after quarter. I was so preoccupied that I didn't care which route I took. I was so agitated that the memory of all my former lovers came back and overwhelmed me.

I went to Marie's and asked after her. The concierge told me, "She sold her place a long time ago. I don't know where she is."

I was too upset to find a new place to worry. I went back home hoping that Léon had returned, that everything had been taken care of. I went downstairs twenty times. I spent the night watching, listening. It was torture, a melodrama that lasted twelve hours. The fear of being the cause of a man's death filled me with dread.

The bells rang out six in the morning. It made me shiver and shake. I had lasted the October night. I think this was a premonition that everything was finished. I paced. I went back and forth to the window. I saw a coach coming along fauborg Saint-Honoré. Without seeing the face of whoever was inside, I threw myself down the stairs. I came to the door as the coach pulled up.

It was Léon!

I threw my arms around his neck. He pushed me into the entryway. "Are you insane? It's cold, and you're only wearing a muslin nightgown."

I pulled him up to my rooms, saying, "I am so happy to see you! I was so scared!"

He was wearing a black button-up shirt, black trousers, and stockings. He was so elegant, even when wearing an exaggerated version of the English fashion. It wasn't too bad on him. That day, I found everything about him good. He was pale, he was cold. I tried to warm his hands in mine. I asked how it all happened.

"It went well for everyone," he said. "We both shot so poorly that there was more danger for the witnesses than for us."

"You really did shoot?"

"Oui."

He seemed like a great man to me. I asked the name of his adversary. He refused to tell me, begging me not to speak of the encounter to anyone.

When I had calmed my nerves, I thought again of the whole story. I couldn't help but smile, and I remembered the order to keep quiet. He was so talkative that we often quarreled over the stupid lies he invented.

Over the next few days, I saw many of his friends, who seemed to me completely ignorant of this duel, which I found surprising. I tried to learn more on the sly. Word of an argument in a full café would get around quickly, but no one had any knowledge of it. Suspecting that he had lied to me, I promised to clear my own conscience. I found it repellant to make light of reason and honor.

The Hippodrome put on one of its last shows for the season. The dry leaves that had fallen in the arena crunched under the horses' hooves like black ice. Everyone's zeal had cooled; the audience had red noses. It was time to end it.

The day of the final show, it began to rain so hard that the clay created seas of water at both ends of the grounds. There was hardly anyone there, but when there was a show to put on, it was tough for even one person to ride, to make a go of it.

On this day, I had friends in the audience. I saw Pomaré, and I wanted to win my race. We were advised to go easy because the track was so bad, but as soon as we took off, I pushed my horse. The others did the same, and we flew like starlings.

At the first corner, we heard someone yell that a horse had fallen. That didn't stop us. I was in second place, and the rider in front of me was Coralie. She too seemed to have some reason to win, because she gripped her reins so hard she couldn't let go, and she kept me from passing her. Her horse made a mistake and she corrected it, but she lost half a second, and I took advantage. We rode over the line neck and neck.

There was a lot of applause. The other riders were taken off the course, and Coralie and I did another lap.

We again took off together. Coming to the first turn, I don't know which of us got too close to the other, but our horses collided. We rolled on for a bit in the white, runny mud. Coralie was thrown off her horse head-first. When I saw her legs go over her head, I completely forgot to wonder if she was hurt. I began to laugh so hard that she joined in. Everyone could see that we were fine. You wouldn't call our cuts and bruises bad.

We wanted to restart, but we were told, "Enough!"

We got the bouquets, and we went backstage covered

in mud and glory.

I dined that evening at café Foy with Léon and his friends. They spoke first of my tumble, then they began to tease Léon. There's always a target in these circles, and it's almost always the one who's paying the bill. It seemed that the ridicule they threw his way usually landed on me. I often defended him, and since I had enough wit to hold their attention, once I began, they finished with me. They always picked up on something unsavory.

That evening, heads were hot. Everyone wanted to be funny at someone else's expense, and they chose Léon. I never participated in these pile-ons. I held my own, and insults never stopped me.

"That's it, gentlemen," I said. "Every time we dine together, you say the same things. Even if Léon doesn't pay for the mood, he always pays the bill. If he foots this expense to learn something, you best be funny and have something new every time. If not, we'll swap you out."

They began to laugh, but the laughter turned bitter. The most irritated was a tall, blond young man, thin and nice enough looking. Instead of a tie, he wore ribbons around his neck that he said he'd asked women for as tokens to remember them. But really it was to save money. He's like all those who aspire to be high class. You often find him at the door of famous cafes. He's never hungry, but he comes in just to say hello to someone who asked him in. And then he eats enough for four. He's an office worker, he earns 1,200 francs. Thanks to this little game, he lives as if he had 100,000 livres. He scorns women who don't have a carriage. He is crude toward everyone. He doesn't tip his hat for fear of wearing it out; he just makes a little wave with his hand. A pretty actress—that is to say, a good actress at the Palais-Royal—falls in love with him. One evening when she's at his place, she realizes she doesn't have any money on her, so she asks him for two francs to pay for her carriage. A week later, she puts her money on the mantel, and he takes back his forty sous. Poverty is not a sin, but pride and stinginess are neither interesting nor dignified, and I don't indulge them.

Irritated that Léon didn't have any response, I said to him, "My dear, instead of being carried away by people insulting me and getting yourself into a duel, be a man and spare yourself these tasteless jokes."

Everyone looked at him. He turned purple.

"Who? Him, duel?" said one of his friends. "When? Where? With who?"

"I have no idea. He didn't want to tell me."

Léon was crimson. I felt a wave of regret pass over me for having said anything. He stammered. He had lied to me, but to what end? A history of lying. This disgusted me.

He became fodder for gossip, and he left Paris for the country. I gladly accepted my freedom from him.

∽

The duke was in Spain at the time, so I went all over town with Lise. The parties where we had the most fun were always Alphonse R…'s. He had regained his health and happiness. In his house, we were treated like spoiled children. Our parties were more fantastic every day. This circle of spirited people was infinitely fun.

I kept my ears open, and my intellect grew from this contact. I was in desperate need of it, because I was so ignorant that I often stopped myself short in the middle of a word that I didn't dare finish in case I said something stupid. Everyone helped me a little and with so much goodwill that I always remembered it.

Well, the men did. The women were impossible and got on my last nerve.

Once one of these women remarked that Pomaré was not pretty, that she had buck teeth. Her own were only slightly less so. I asked my friend Hermance who this great plank of an exhuasting woman was.

"Her name is Lagie."

"She's pretty, but she's boring. I'm going to give myself the pleasure of telling her so."

Hermance laughed. "Wait a minute; I'll tell you all you need to know. She comes from Metz, and a whole garrison was distraught at her departure. The regiments didn't change often enough for her, so she came here. She's a fine girl, she's just dimwitted and flighty. One day, she's plying you with compliments, the next she doesn't even see you. She never varies in her accounts of women: she talks shit about everyone."

"Good to know. Do me a favor: go tell her, for me, that I would like to make her acquaintance."

"Why?"

"To find out if she wants peace or war."

Hermance went off on her mission. I saw in the way she was received that Mlle Lagie found me very bold. I put up my guard.

After about a week, I had so mocked her, scoffed at her, and bored her that she invited me to dinner. She lived lavishly and loved to spend money on a whim.

A scion of Albion showered her in a rain of gold, so it didn't matter to her if the sun rose the next day. Nothing was good enough for her. Her dinners were sumptuous. She had random friends and was surrounded by a crowd of spongers who approved every stupid thing she said or did.

On the day I went to dinner with her, there were a lot of people there. Someone rang while the soup was being served, and Lagie signaled to all the revelers to be quiet. She was afraid it was her Englishman.

Instead of obeying her request, some jokers began to sing at the top of their lungs:

War to tyrants!
Never, never in France,
Never will the English reign there.
The irreverent Lagie sang along with them.

We heard someone in the square speaking, and it ended with "Goddamn!" Everyone present laughed about it all night. But the next day, they realized they didn't know how they'd pay for dinner anymore. The Englishman had left for good.

❧

Lise and I kept our promise to M. H…, and we went to spend the evening at his house. I gambled sometimes, but I'd never had a taste for the game. The women who played seemed ghastly to me. It's an obsession that often makes a man ugly and always makes a woman ugly.

H… was seated next to me, and he gave me advice. He was more occupied with me than with the game. Everything I know about gambling is thanks to him; at that time, after music, cards were his great passion.

My disdain for gambling didn't discourage him.

He had a relentless persistence in his love. I told him, "Look, H..., you're a good man. I don't want to push you away, but don't be in love with me, or don't love me more than you already do, because I can't return your affections. I'm glad to be your friend, but I could never love you. And you must want better than me. I would cause you grief at every turn. You're jealous enough now; what would it be like if you had any right to be jealous?"

"I swear to you, Céleste," he told me with animated seriousness, "that it's not my fault that I'm Jewish. If one were born in the age of man and able to choose his religion, I would be Catholic to make you happy."

While I was teasing him, a newcomer entered and came over to the master of the house to pay his respects. I let out a cry and lowered my head to hide the blush that came to my cheeks with such force it felt like blood would come out my eyes.

H... clasped my hand without understanding. He looked at me and then at the newcomer.

I raised my head at last, hoping I was mistaken. But it was no other. The man who stood before me, looking at me with a dull eye, was the one I've wrote about when I first entered the bordello, my Amphitryon from Rocher de Cancale.

He was about to say aloud where he knew me from but realized all his friends would look down on me. I leaned on H...'s shoulder as if to say to him, *Protect me!* I pulled myself together and looked the enemy in the face to better read his mind. I didn't see anything cross this impenetrable screen, which looked like death or sleep. He took a few steps and went to sit down some distance away without letting on that he recognized me.

My heart had a flash of insight—I couldn't lose sight

of him. Each time that he spoke to someone, my ears rang. It seemed as if H… could hear it too.

"Do you know him?" H… asked me.

"No!" I said so quickly that, for a jealous man, it was as good as a yes.

H… got up after several minutes and went to chat with his friend. I lost my composure.

A young man came to take H…'s seat. He spoke to me, but I didn't hear him. All my attention was concentrated on the small group where H… was chatting with the newcomer. Luckily he spoke a little loudly, and he wasn't talking about me. I began to breathe again, and I could answer my neighbor.

"You're not being kind," he was saying. "Poor H… is crazy in love with you. You want to make him stop, but you're making him miserable. It's not how a good girl behaves."

"Like you're any better! By your count, to be a good girl, you have to give yourself to all who want you. But, my dear, I'm on my tenth lover for the evening. What should I do if I'm obligated to be a good girl with all of them?"

"You're right. It's true that it's hard to watch you speaking with all these men without conceding your point, but I'm not convinced. Of the ten people who have made a declaration of love to you this evening, nine won't think of you tomorrow. While H…—that's something else. He's heartsick. He is so good. So sweet."

"Are you serious?"

"Very serious."

That's how this world works. Even the uninvolved favor these liaisons. It seems like nothing could be more frivolous, but payback is on the horizon. For the gentleman involved, it's only a temporary connection, formed on a whim, that can be undone by boredom. For the woman, it's an obstacle that trips up her entire existence. The clock chimes for everyone—sometimes for the lover, sometimes for the mistress. She comes through this whirlpool with a smile on her lips and flowers in her hair, but the only way out is her downfall—this one into misery, that one into despair. This one goes to the cloisters, that one to the morgue.

My relationship with H... is a pathetic example of the dangers of passion. In thinking I was satisfying a whim, I may have changed his life.

The time came to leave the party. The guests picked up their hats, their coats. I remained seated. Everyone looked at me in surprise.

"You're not coming?" Lise said.

"No, I'm staying."

I thought that H... was gong to lose his mind with joy. To steer his guests out more quickly, he shoved them on the shoulders.

Don't be scared off, dear reader! I promised you I'd write the truth, and I'll keep my word.

If I recall that night correctly, I was able to do it without hurting his modesty. But maybe it's you who are to blame, and your imagination has already gone too far. Too bad for you.

I leaned over the grand piano, which was covered with the beginnings of songs. I looked at H... when he came back into the room. He wanted to kiss me, but I stopped him.

"Wait, H.... If you're reasonable, you'll come to my place. I am not toying with you, but I will haunt you if you love me."

"Fine with me. I'd give my life to have you to myself, if only for a day." I realized he meant what he said. His eyes shone, his lips glistened.

I pointed him toward the piano bench. He sat down and kissed my hand.

I stretched out in an armchair next to him. He played with such soul and improvised such pretty things that my heart filled.

"I am," he said, "between the two great loves of my life."

He became handsome. His music had harmonies so sweet it resembled hymns. These religious airs—though maybe a little trite—overwhelmed my senses.

Little by little, he seemed to forget about me. I woke up at dawn in the chair where I had fallen asleep. He had noted on lined paper the music that he composed during the night. I stretched my arms, stiff with fatigue, and asked his forgiveness for having kept him from going to bed. He thanked me, as my presence brought him good luck. I was aware of a sweet and respectful affection in him. I promised to spend the night with him.

This sweetness and reserve didn't last long.

I would advise any woman to cultivate sang-froid when loving an artist. After some time, I no longer knew which saint I should pray to.

H…'s love grew every day. He tormented himself to the point of making himself sick. He followed me everywhere and spent nights outside my door. People saw the change in him and blamed me. He could no longer work unless I told him to.

"Have mercy," he repeated endlessly, "have mercy on me! It won't be long. I no longer have any will to live left. Tell me that you hate me, and I'll kill myself to spare you the inconvenience. This kind of life might be fine for everyone else. But it makes me give up hope."

He had clammy skin, and he coughed a lot. They said he had an infection in his lungs. This scared me. *My God*, I said to myself, *if he dies of sorrow!* I did my best to console him. But great lovers are demanding, and I did a poor job of it.

When he did happen to create music, it was melancholy. His piano was more like a church organ.

Once he stopped playing and said to me, "If I weren't a Jew, you would love me, wouldn't you? If I knew, I would renounce my God for your love."

"My poor friend, you are delirious. I don't want even the smallest sacrifice. What could I offer in return? I told you: don't love me, I'll do you wrong. I'm not mistaken—you've gone mad. You don't do anything anymore. They say it's my fault."

"They shouldn't blame you at all. I feel that my life is withering away. I don't have long to live. Let me be happy in my way."

He was so sad that I avoided him as much as I could.

One day, I saw him enter the church of the Madeleine. He stayed in there two hours. He became more and more somber.

Everyone told me to end it. It was better to make a great bonfire that would cure him, they said, than to let him die in a tiny fire.

At last Lise charged herself with telling him what I had decided, due to my affection for him. He began to weep in my apartment and went downstairs with her. She said that she left him at the door of a church, where he went inside.

Some days later, I received a letter in which he told me that his life was no longer his own. He'd put all his confidence in God, who consoled all his sorrows. This was of such great magnitude, of such high-mindedness, that I wanted to ask his forgiveness.

He refused to see me. I assumed he had a mistress, and I berated myself for my gullibility.

❧

The duke returned to Paris. He looked nothing like H… and didn't exhaust me with his love. For him, I was fashionable. He was rich: trends came straight to him. My apartment was so high, and he had such a small foot, that to accommodate him I had to move. I went to live on the second floor at no. 5 rue de l'Arcade, 1,200 francs to rent.

My new apartment had a salon with furniture upholstered in velvet and a piano. This was due to my hiring a piano teacher. His name was Pederlini; he was Italian and patient. I will never be rich enough to pay him what he was worth.

The duke came to see me every two or three days. He never said more than four words to me. I didn't really know why he continued visiting me. I think it was because his friends thought well of me and came to see me often. They told him, "When you get bored with her, we're going to fight about who comes next in line after you." In the spirit of contrariness, he made them wait.

Sometimes I went to l'Opera, where I was always bored. My piano instructor told me that one of his colleagues was going to debut. He had a magnificent voice, but he had a lot of trouble because he didn't speak French. He had been taught *Lucie de Lammermoor* by heart. "I'm accompanying him. I've spoken often of you, and he would love to meet you."

"Why?"

"Because he finds the French very charming—and because he's seen you at the Hippodrome."

"Well then, if he's already seen me, he should be satisfied."

"It seems not. He wants me to introduce you to him, surely to chat with you."

I played a scale wrong, and it grated at his ears. "Fine. I do idiotic things, and you tell him. What kind of conversation would you like me to have with your friend? You keep saying that he doesn't know a word of French. Do you think I'm going to sing *Lucie* so he can understand?"

My instructor was timid. He didn't mention it again.

"Well," I said after my lesson, "bring me your singer. You will serve as his interpreter. Come at noon for one hour. I'm always available then."

"Is tomorrow all right?" he asked, jumping for joy.

"What a child you are! Fine, so be it. Tomorrow."

※

As soon as I woke up, I chastised myself for having consented. I was paying for my rejection of artists, but the loneliness the duke left me in was weighing on me. I was bored, and when bored, you easily accept any excuse to make new acquaintances. The duke had an ex longtime mistress who was fat and awkward. I saw her show out for her fortieth birthday in a beautiful double carriage trimmed in blue velour. She grimaced to make it seem like she was smiling. Her whole face was covered by a dotted black veil, which she took care to never push aside.

So I got up, without too much regret, and dressed in my best to receive my two Italians.

The noon bell and a knock on my door sounded at the same time. I went to open the door.

My antechamber was dim. I saw the shadow of a tall figure looming over the head of my pianist.

"Excuse me for coming so early," Pederlini said, "but it was not at all my fault. Ever since I promised to bring B… to your house, he hasn't given me a minute's rest. If I'd listened to him, we would have come at eight o'clock this morning."

I showed them to two chairs in the salon then sat facing them. My new admirer was a handsome man—tall and strong, with large, shining black eyes that fixed me with such an expression that I automatically lowered my head under his gaze.

He spoke to Pederlini, who translated. "He says you're even prettier up close."

I raised my eyes to thank him, but I had to lower them again even faster than the first time. I began to play with the ring on my finger, turning it to calm myself down. "So, you don't speak any French?" I said.

"Si, un poco, Céleste."

"You know how to say my name?"

"I thought it would be good," said Pederlini. "There was enough time for him to learn that. He does know how to speak a little French, but you intimidate him."

I wanted to answer that it was him who intimidated me.

B… offered to teach me Italian, and I might do him the favor of teaching him French. He promised to work hard so he could chat with me and tell me all that he was thinking. I hurried him along, because we must have seemed very stupid, the way we were speaking.

At the end of our hour, they stood to leave. B… held my hand and squeezed it with such force that for a few seconds I was powerless to release my fingers from the pain. I don't know if that's the Italian way; I found it rough. Then I thought he might mean it as an enthusiastic mark of affection.

B… had a truly kind nature, with his flawless skin, red lips, white teeth, his frank demeanor, and his fiery gaze. When I compared him to the duke—so blond, so cold, so calm—the advantage was to Italy over Spain. But the duke flattered my vanity. When his beautiful coach arrived at my door, I was proud of the very thing that should have made both of us blush.

The duke arrived while I was still under the effects of the previous visitor.

"What's going on, my dear? You're very distracted."

"Oui," I said, a little evasively. I've always abhorred lying.

"What is it?"

"I'm bored here all day. I want to go out sometimes."

"Why didn't you say something?" he said in the same tone as always. "Tomorrow I will come fetch you in a coach."

I jumped for joy. I couldn't sleep all night.

At four o'clock, a lovely coach with two horses stopped at my door. The coachman came to tell me he was at my service.

I went out and only came home when the streets were deserted. I was so tired that I couldn't eat. The fear that I wouldn't be seen inside the back of the coach made me sit at the edge of my seat, face at the window, moving my head about like a porcelain doll. Then I was afraid of being accused of being proud.

The next day, the same scene—only I had moved up the hour of my sojourn, and I was disappointed to find the Champs-Élysées empty. Still, I didn't want to get out of the coach. If the coachman hadn't let me know his horses were hungry, I would have ridden around in it all night.

The day after that, all this ridiculous vanity fell away and good sense returned. I knocked myself down a peg by telling myself very loudly and very often that all these luxuries were passing and that this coach, which I was so proud of, didn't belong to me. A whim had given it to me, and a whim could take it back.

※

I went several days without seeing the Italian, who was busy preparing for his debut. I wasn't angry. It didn't take long for communicating via gazes and conversation via interpreter to get old. It was definitely going better now that he'd had time to make progress in learning French.

Inside the bohemian scene, as in other countries of the world, it is not always prudent to render services there. When it came to the duke and B…, I put this to the test.

One day while I was riding along the boulevard du Temple, I saw a girl I had known at the Beaumarchais theater pass by. I pulled the cord to stop the carriage and called to her. Since she had nothing to do that day, I brought her along to dinner. She was about twenty, tall and not badly put together, pretty, with rosy cheeks. I knew she was on the spirited side, but I thought that was good.

"Well, my poor Josephine," I said when she was

seated next to me, "what have you been doing since I last saw you? Are you happy?"

"Non. I could be happy if I wanted, but I'm not, thanks to my own stupidity. I have an obsession that's eating me up. It began with my dresses and ended with my furniture. Now I no longer have anything. *He* doesn't want to see me anymore. He told me that I disgust him, with my big feet and large hands." The fact is that in this area, nature had been a little too liberal with her.

"What devil are you so wild about?"

"An actor! I am an extra in *Délassements* because of my love."

"Well, you have to quit *Délassements*, of course. Do you want to go back to the Hippodrome? I would put in a word for you. Do you want to stay with me? I'll help you forget your lover. It's stupid to love a guy like that!"

We had dinner. I dressed her from head to toe, and I brought her to l'Opera to see *Robert le Diable*. I introduced her to the duke and his friends, who took us for ice cream at café Anglais.

Josephine seemed to find this kind of life very agreeable. She hung onto me and made the most beautiful declarations of friendship.

⁂

The debut of B… was announced.

I dined out that day and arrived late at the theater. The noise from the box as the curtain opened made me raise my head toward my tenor. He had to sing the passage from *Lucie*, "Céleste providence"!

I can see him still. He opened his arms, looked toward me, and stopped short on the word "Céleste."

This lasted two or three seconds, not long enough for anyone else to notice.

Pederlini came over during the entr'acte to tell me that he was worried and that he was very sorry that I was there. I was going to distract B…. I offered to leave so as to not bother the poor boy.

"Non," he said, "I think the worst has already happened. He'll be looking for you. Your leaving would be even worse."

"How handsome he is!" my friend said, marveling at B…'s black velvet suit. She complimented his singing in the first act.

B… undoubtedly thought his good performance was due to my being there, because he seemed to thank me with a look as he retook the stage. He wanted to do well so badly that he sang a wrong note.

He tried to collect himself in the third act, but his voice was weak. The stress of performing in his debut had made his voice a little hoarse. At the end of the scene, I thought he might be dying; it sounded like his death rattle.

I was devastated for him. He was such a beautiful boy that before he'd even opened his mouth, he already had enemies in the room. They didn't hiss; they laughed. A few people made fun of him. He had a noticeable accent, so they called him Gascon, or Auvergnat.

If this went well, he would get forty thousand francs a year! I knew how much he must be hurting, and I wanted to tell him that much of it was my fault, that he shouldn't be discouraged, that he still had two more performances as part of his debut.

After the performance, Pederlini took my hand and led me to B…. He wasn't too upset. I gently told him which words he'd pronounced incorrectly, and I made him repeat them many times.

"Now that you've started these lessons, you must continue," Pederlini said to me, laughing. "I'm sure he'll make great progress with you."

B... seemed to agree, because he came to take as many as two lessons a day.

At his second debut, I was pale as death. I was so nervous, I was shaking on his behalf.

He sang better this time, and he pretended that this was because of me. He didn't want to leave my side, saying that I was indispensable to him and he wanted to prove that he knew it. He gave a grand dinner in my honor and to celebrate his debuts.

His third debut was entirely successful, and B... was on cloud nine. His happiness lifted his spirits.

You don't know what you're getting into when you catch the attention of an Italian.

⁂

I had gotten Josephine work at the Hippodrome. We returned to working together. I learned a new act—they now had chariots driven by women. There were three of us who would race: Angèle, Louise, and me.

I lived in complete security, without any clue about the danger that threatened me. Josephine was a snake that I had coddled in my cashmere. This dear friend figured out that she had owed me for a long time, and the moment had come to prove her gratitude. She could think of no better way to do it than by replacing me in the duke's affections.

One lovely morning she came into my bedroom to get ready, with a shawl and a hat that she borrowed from me, then drove to the duke's residence. He refused to see her at first, but she was so persistent that he gave in.

What she told him, I'll never know. He knew better than to explain the cancan to me. She came back to my place after making him promise to keep her visit a secret. She had surely received a few louis for her treachery.

The duke came to see me at four o'clock the same day. He spoke to me of l'Opera and the singers. I understood that I had been on someone's tongue.

Josephine didn't even turn pink. When he'd left, she said she had no idea how he knew all that.

But I'd seen her signal to him in a mirror. I had no doubt about her backstabbing.

It was never my way to negotiate. I could see perfectly well that it was over between the duke and me. I didn't have any wish to humiliate myself to get back into his good graces, but I wanted justice from Josephine.

I wrote the duke asking him to come speak to me the next day and saying that he could withdraw his friendship after. But I wished to have one last interview with him.

His carriage arrived exactly on time, to the great regret of my dear friend Josephine, who had been ill at ease since the day before. She wanted to leave, but I begged her to do nothing of the sort. She insisted, so I forbade her.

"You'll leave in a few minutes. I want to have my heart cleared of suspicions."

She pulled herself together with incredible aplomb.

I didn't have time to say any more, because just then the duke entered.

"You are very kind to come; thank you," I said. "I don't want to force you to do anything. If you no longer wish to see me, I won't do anything to change your mind. It may be that I've done all that people told you, or it may be that they're exaggerating quite a bit. I could try to justify myself, but if your intention is to end it, that would merely bore you without convincing you. I only want to know the author of these lovely stories. I only see one woman who was in a position to harm your opinion of me: Josephine. But I can't believe it could be her, since without me she wouldn't know where to eat and likely would set up on a streetcorner to offer her beauty to passersby. Look, I don't want to lie to you. She has my stockings on her legs. She would also be wearing my slippers if she didn't have such big feet. She wears my chemises, my dresses, my collars. I've fed her for several months, I've gotten work for her, I've shared with her all that I have. If it was her, admit that this would be very bad and that I was right to ask you to come so I could tell her, in front of you, 'You are the most despicable person in the world. Get out of my house. Your backstabbing will do you no good.'"

I became more and more intense. Josephine didn't move. She was sure the duke would protect her, but he did have a fair mind and straightforward heart. The scorn that he had for me did not prevent him from understanding my indignation toward Josephine. Seeing me white with anger, he asked me to go into my bedroom. He followed and made every effort to calm me down. Then he rang for my maid and ordered her to send away Mlle Josephine, who must not stay another minute in my apartment.

When Josephine had left, he told me that he wanted to spare my pride, that he would always be my friend, that if I ever needed him, I only had to write. He told me he was leaving for the country but didn't say when he'd be back.

I understood that this was a dismissal. In my mind, I had already taken my leave of him, yet I was sad for several days. There's no link, however small, that doesn't require effort to break. In spite of all my beautiful plans, I couldn't go on without grieving for my life of ease and luxury. I found myself newly exposed to the vagaries of discomfort and the unexpected.

I was astonished to see the carriage come the next morning as usual. The coachman told me that he'd been paid three months in advance. In the midst of my financial disaster, it should have been egregious of me to maintain the remnants of my past splendor for a few extra days. I had the childishness to swear otherwise and the pleasure of riding in a coach to help me heal my wounds more quickly.

I was bored being alone. I went to dinner almost every day at B…'s. It was definitely not gourmet. I could never stand macaroni, and that was the extent of the cuisine. I hate cheese, and it was everywhere. But I found a lot of company there. We sang, we made beautiful music. A police officer came, found it too fun, and told us to keep it down.

B… had rented a very nice furnished apartment, no. 10 rue de Richelieu, to be near l'Opera. When he sang with his friends, especially *Belisario*, people gathered in the street and at the corner of the boulevard. The crowd grew so large that carriages couldn't get around. He and his friends decided to close the windows and sing less loudly.

He often showed me letters that someone had written to him speaking ill of me. When a tenor has the bad luck to love someone outside l'Opera, the antagonized rats nibble at their rival until she bleeds. One of those who had a developed a great passion for this singer wrote to him:

How can you be so blind not to see who you love and attach yourself to a woman who doesn't have the status of the horse she rides?

I asked him curtly to keep these love letters to himself and never make me think about them. I wanted to say something I'd read that morning in the newspaper: "Their insults don't rise to the level of my contempt!" But I figured that, being a foreigner, he wouldn't get the nuance.

⁂

The day of the Hippodrome's reopening arrived! The Roman chariots were a huge success. The costumes were magnificent. I had a Phrygian helmet with gold stars, a white tunic embroidered in gold that came to my knees and opened on the side to the hip, red buckskin sandals, a sweeping cape on my right shoulder, and the sleeve of the left shoulder was gathered and held with a brooch. This costume was impossible for other women to wear. Most of my colleagues let out yelps and lengthened their skirts. I neglected to take this precaution.

This act was horribly dangerous and horribly tiring. I went home the day of the premiere with the worst headache. I threw myself on the bed in my house dress.

B…, who had come to compliment me on my success, was distraught to see that I was unwell. He annoyed me with the force of his care and offers of help. I told him there was only one remedy for a migraine: rest. He persisted, which put me in a terrible mood.

There was a ring at the door, and my maid came in, frightened. "Madame, the duke!"

"Oh my God!" I said, surprised. "I don't want him to see you here. Go into the other bedroom."

"That is impossible, madame," said B.... "The duke is in the salon. I would have to walk past him."

I pointed at the door of a small cabinet at the foot of my bed.

He frowned and flatly answered that he did not want to.

"Get in," I said with authority, "or I'll never see you again. I've already risked too much for you. If you don't get in there, I'm going to break up with you in front of him."

We were out of time. The door opened.

"You made me wait in the salon," said the duke as he looked around. "Were you not in here alone?"

"I was," I said, pointing to a footbath near the fireplace. "I didn't want to receive you with bare feet."

"Did something happen? You drove your chariot very well today! That Roman costume looked marvelous on you. I promised my friends I'd bring you to dinner with them this evening."

"I'm sorry to make you go back on your word, but I can't go. The emotional energy and the jolting of the chariot gave me a headache and heartache that make me awful to be around."

"My dear, I promised. You absolutely must come. You can be sick tomorrow."

"I must! You are astounding, you and your other

grand lords. It seems that as soon as you've said the word, all of nature obeys. The dead should rise from their graves and the sick should get well. Nothing could be as charming as declaring, 'You must'! If I were feeling better, this 'you must' alone would be enough to make me refuse. Suppose I could go out; who told you I had no other engagements? For two weeks, you've given me no sign of life. I was free."

"I am rich enough to make you break your word to others. Get dressed and be at café Anglais at six o'clock. Tomorrow I'll bring you a present to make it up to you. Am I to continue to be on my best behavior? Am I to stop paying for your coach? Don't let what you have go."

He left without waiting for my response.

The huge bell of Notre-Dame clanged inside my head. B… came out of his cabinet, his gaze inflamed with rage and fixed on the door.

"You don't need a heart to live like that! When I believed you without a doubt! This man does not love you. He came to see you today because he heard people talking about your grace and elegance. These are the approving murmurs of a public that throws itself at your feet."

"You're not telling me anything I don't know, but what do you want me to do? I told you about it ages ago. Within all the rotten things that he said to me, there's a lot of truth. Don't make things up on my behalf. He provides me with a small fortune so that I can reach a goal that I cannot explain to you. My current financial state is not enough."

"Why not make something of yourself? This life is shameful. If I should ever meet him in person, I would appreciate the woman that I love more than he does. Go to dinner; the order was clear. I will drive you there if you like, and I will say goodbye to you forever at the door."

Though it was said in bad French, all this hurt me to the core. The beating of my heart sounded so fast and deep that B… had to speak loudly to tell me all this. But it wasn't in my nature to give in and give up without answering him.

"Be careful, my friend. You're sure you know how to defeat me, but I am warning you. It's dangerous. You said that if I go to this dinner, you will no longer come see me. I'm not giving in to your threat; I'm not going to dinner because I can't and don't want to. I'll write a polite letter to the duke. If status and wealth made him a spoiled child, it's not his fault. I'm glad for what he wants to do for me. Maybe I'll fight with him a little, but I won't be rude or ungrateful." And I pleaded drily enough that B… let me rest.

❦

The duke came the next day to hear my response. He was cold and glum. Being used to everyone bending to his will, he didn't understand the word *impossible*. I believed nevertheless that because of my personality and how often I resisted his whims, he would have a certain affection for me in the end.

I was brought back down to earth with great disappointment. I saw all around me the rise and fall of all the women like me who had admired me from afar. Nothing is sadder than lovers who begin in the night and end with the day. The smoke clears, reality appears—awful, horrifying! Debt and misery watch the women behind their lace curtains. Old women become entirely destitute.

The young must always have a sparkling wardrobe. If they were to die, you wouldn't find in their armoire a scrap of fabric to enshroud them. And yet, once inside this whirlwind, it is very difficult to get out. It's those women who are the most extravagant. The wise are the insane. The young men want to ride a new horse every day, so the women put on a new dress. Existence is no longer merely defying impossible circumstances. It's a racecourse when the starting bell sounds, a sort of steeplechase where you lose—unless a miracle happens—health, rest, conscience, and honor.

Among all my misfortunes, I had one stroke of luck: the despair, whether moral or physical, always came to wake me up in time and kept me from drinking myself to death, as I saw so many others do. It's the fatal blow of this fake fortune. By the grace of these interventions, which saved me from torturing myself, I could keep one thing intact, along with the qualities that the good Lord had placed in my heart: energy!

A massive depression came to distract me from discouragement when I was near to letting myself drag to the ground.

⁕

Nothing is as contagious as a fad. That year, because of the shows at the Hippodrome, there was a huge rage for horseback riding. All the women rode horses and looked for things to jump over in order to be like us. Not being able to drive chariots, they began to drive their own coaches.

Lise often rode a horse. She was so happy. She had an apartment, no. 33 rue Saint-Georges. She had also been thrown into a fiery love affair. Her new lover was the comte de ***. She had said that as soon as she moved in, she'd write to me. She never kept her promise.

One day, as I was leaving the Hippodrome, I saw people congregating in groups. An accident must have happened. I went to see.

"Could you tell me what happened, monsieur, please?"

"An accident that would be horrible if it happened to anyone else, but this one's no great loss."

I looked at the man. I had the feeling that I was going to be sorry, but I had to know. "What happened?" I said.

"She embarrassed herself among the coaches," he said, half laughing. "Her horse got frightened and took off, and no one tried to stop it. Her hair was all over the place, and she looked insane."

Other people who had come to the barrier after me said, "The poor woman. She wanted to jump off the horse, but her foot was caught in the stirrup. The horse dragged her so far that her head was mutilated. It's awful to think about. You couldn't make out her face. She had a mask of blood and hair."

I jumped into my carriage and drove in the direction they had pointed. Groups clustered around splotches of blood in the street. The unfortunate woman had been taken away, and no one had identified her. I said to the coachman, "Rue Saint-Georges!"

Her maid told me that Lise had gone out that morning in city clothes. This was meaningless, because her riding dress was at the riding school. I said that I was going to the school at rue Duphot, and if there was news, they should send it to my house as soon as possible.

I was assured at the riding school that they hadn't seen Lise all day. They showed me her dress hanging where it belonged. I went back home to change because I was drenched in sweat. I was about to go out again when someone rang.

"It's her! I'm sure of it." I said to myself as I passed before my mirror while getting dressed. I often had these visions, and they never failed me.

I went to open my door and my arms. When I had embraced Lise enough, I told her the rumors that were running around, and the fear that I'd had. I wouldn't leave her side for two days.

The unlucky woman who had fallen from her horse died from her wounds.

Lise told me about her love, named Ernest, and she introduced me to him at dinner. Her sister Eulalie was pregnant and had come to live with her so she could be better cared for. All four of us dined together.

M. Ernest was a man of forty-five, blond but half bald. He combed his hair over his head to hide the bald spot. His face was long and narrow, so he kept his sideburns long to hide the wrinkles in his cheeks. He was short and thin, and his skin was both sallow and seemed too big for his face, as it pooled in folds. His eyes were a faded blue, his mouth was large, and his nose narrow. His mustache was reddish-blond, and he had excellent teeth. I'm irritated that I have to say anything nice at all about him because I did not like him.

Lise had said nothing but good things about his generosity, his love for her. I could never get past this first impression. To not cause him grief, as she seemed to owe something to this particular species of monkey, I found him charming.

Eulalie was near her due date, and she made a layette for Lise, who was to be godmother. They had bought a small cradle. Camille had asked to be godfather. He was still the same, and Lise had begun to count on him.

She told me of a ball she had to go to in Passy at some young men's house. She asked me if I would go, if I wanted to take her. I said yes, but since it was a week away, she could let me know if she changed her mind.

The week went by without any word, so I went to her place at two o'clock.

"Still coming?" I asked.

"Certainly," she said. "Come in. I'm arranging flowers in my hair."

I went into her room, which was lit with candles. Her sister slept on a divan that served as her bed.

"Are you ill?" I asked Lise, seeing how pale she was.

"Yes," she said, "but it's nothing. Hold on—I'm going to put these pomegranates there."

I examined the other flowers strewn on the little cradle. I felt something like the head of an infant. I recoiled a little and saw a small cross and blessed casket. I returned to myself, shaken.

"What is going on here?"

"You can see for yourself: my sister had a miscarriage last night. It was a girl. She can't be buried until tomorrow."

I backed out of the room, saying to Lise, "Come get me when you're ready. I'm not coming back here."

She arrived that evening, all done up, without seeming to think about the fact that she had left the dead at her house. She was full of strange contradictions. Her insensitivity in this situation astonished me. I recalled the despair that she had shown at the death of her own child, and I thought this event would have renewed her depression.

I don't know, maybe it was just a given in the circles I moved in, but it seemed I'd never experienced anything else in this life: thoughtlessness, everywhere and always. Maybe that's lucky. There are such atrocious things in the human species that if it were always in agreement with itself, it would be horrible!

15.

A Chariot Race

I RETURNED TO THE BALL under the least auspicious of circumstances.

We were in the first days of July, and the heat was oppressive, which made my work at the Hippodrome exhausting. I had already had two or three falls with my horse, and I'd been bloodied twice, which tired me out. I slept badly at night. I had a thousand bad dreams. I woke up depressed and anxious.

One morning, I opened my window and checked the weather. It was lovely. The sun was shining, which usually cheered me up and brought me back to life. Yet my heart was clenched like a fist. I sat at the table unable to eat.

"Is madame ill?" asked my maid.

"Ill, non. But I feel like I'm about to hear bad news. I have death in my soul. It's the Hippodrome. I'm going to break my neck today."

"It's a shameful kind of work you do there."

She was right, because I earned so little. I decided to ask for a raise. Would they give it to me? They had more women than they needed; to state the obvious, these women offered themselves for nothing. They'd never even taken a riding lesson, but what was that to the people who ran the show, who made a fortune? They scorned those women who made their own money. If the inspectors didn't keep an eye on the show, the owners would have killed four out of ten riders. Does a spectacle without danger have any draw? They never tried to prevent accidents. They gave us horses with bad legs who lost their footing as soon as you pressed them to go faster.

In making the Cross of Berny, which was one of our acts, an Englishman fell, along with his horse, into the hole in the center. This hole was about a dozen feet deep. Everyone thought the man and horse had died, because neither climbed out. But the man had only fainted. When he came to, he had a large, gaping would on his forehead. The doctor ordered him to bed immediately. One of the directors who was there when he fell, and who seemed to be especially worried about this trick being forbidden due to how dangerous it was, said, "Put him on a stretcher and take him to the hospital." Just then the poor, wounded man opened his eyes, clasped his hands, and begged them to let him die right there rather than carry him off to the hospital. I don't know why the hospital scared him so, and I didn't ask. But since no one said anything, I couldn't contain myself.

"Bullshit!" I said. "This is the fate that awaits us if we don't have resources. It's not enough that we have to cancel our appointments when we're sick, we also have worry that a fall like this won't immediately kill us. Drive this miserable man to my house. I'll take care of him to put these bastards to shame."

The poor boy kissed my hands. Everyone looked at me approvingly. One of the directors, Laloue, said I was right and gave the order to take the wounded man to his house instead. He was a good soul, whom God has since called home. He'd had a hard life, but he had a superior mind. The name of Ferdinand Laloue remained in the memory of those he worked with and those who knew him well.

The poor Englishman was wrecked. He had a flattened nose, a scar along his cheek, and five broken teeth.

To do the Cross of Berny, you need good riders. Since the good ones were expensive, we took the bad ones who couldn't ride steady. They were always tipsy, lived in squalid rooms, didn't have friends, and had been forgotten by society. Maybe that's what made them dread the hospital.

※

Five days later, they had me try out a horse for the steeplechase. To train a horse, we jockeys would ride on either side of me. These two were blind drunk. They left such a huge gap between our horses that my horse took off on his own for eight or ten laps with me helpless on his back. I jumped twenty gates, each three and a half feet high. My palms were bloody from clutching the reins. The jockeys were fined, but their drunkenness could have cost me my life. My horse made mistakes at every jump.

They found this funny and went off to laugh about it at the wine shop. I didn't show such lightheartedness. If I could have, I would have left the Hippodrome without regret.

I was done testing the horse by one o'clock, but I was upset. When I finally got to my dressing room, I was able to laugh with my friends. The first part of the day was over. I rode in two sets, and I was more confident in the performance each time.

I said to Angèle and Louise, "Don't squeeze my horse in too much. I've been feeling off all morning."

"The day's half over. The rest will go fine," said Angèle. "But there are days like this."

We did a lap in our chariots to get to the starting line. As we lined up, they yelled, "Go!"

My heart constricted, but when I was carried along like the wind, I lost my fear. The race promised to be good. The chariots overtook each other lap after lap. I passed Louise, and I went to pass Angèle on the last lap.

In the corner, near the box seats, I saw that Louise was coming in close at my side. I went to whip my horse to spur him on when I felt a violent jolt.

Louise had caught one of the protrusions from the back of my chariot in her wheel, the piece of wood that keeps the chassis from dragging on the ground. If she'd have stopped short, this stud could have gotten free of her wheel, but she whipped her horse to pass me and dragged me along. My chariot spun, and its shaft hit my horse. He reared up against a pole, let out a whinny that cut the air, and came down backward. In his fall, he dragged down the other horse. But that horse, in trying to remain upright, pulled to the side and caused my chariot to tip over.

I still held the reins to keep the horse from getting free and dragging me along. But another horse that was thrashing about hit me in the shoulder. I loosened my grip and was filled with fear. I only heard chaotic noise around me.

"She's dead!"

The horse made an effort to get free and dragged me a few steps with my face against the ground. Something ran over my leg twice. I screamed and thought my back was broken.

They stopped the thrashing horses. One had a broken leg; he had to be put down to stop his screams. This scene must have been horrifying for the audience. Some women were crying, others fainted. The crowd scaled the barriers and questioned the doctors who surrounded me.

I opened my eyes, got to my knees, and then stood. I passed my hand along my right thigh and felt a great pain, but I stayed upright. My legs weren't broken, as I'd thought. I pushed everyone aside. I wanted to try to walk to assure myself that I didn't have anything else broken. I succeeded, but in the worst pain and leaving a trail of blood behind me.

I waved to the public, who had come because they were interested in seeing me, and I wanted to reassure them. I took a few steps while being held up beneath my arms, then I collapsed into a heap.

I was brought around, and they cleaned me up twice. The blood wouldn't stop.

They bandaged me and stretched me out in the back of a carriage. The coachman was ordered to go slow. Some women followed me, though I'm not sure whether it was out of concern for me or to make sure they were seen being concerned for me. This pathetic cortege grew along the route as the curious joined. Each gave their opinion. In the end, they were saying, "She's a goner!"

I couldn't at all deny their assumption. My body was stiff, cold. My heart didn't seem to be beating anymore. This didn't cause me any grief; on the contrary, I thanked God. I had come so far in such a short time, but no one loved me.

When I'd been brought upstairs and put into my bed, I closed my eyes and waited for the end. Fever overtook me.

❦

The next day, I came out of this numbness. I examined my injuries. Half my shoulder and my elbow were abraded. Grains of sand from the track had gotten into the chariot and made holes in my flesh.

To keep the chariots from going too fast in the corners, they had filled the wheels with lead. One of these wheels had passed over my thigh and marked it with violet flesh as wide as my hand. I had a dislocated knee that bulged under the kneecap. I had a two-inch-long cut over my thigh bone that had undoubtedly been made by an iron-shod horse as he thrashed about. My leg was on fire.

The Hippodrome's doctor came to see me. He ordered rest and compresses. I followed his prescriptions for six days without getting better. On the contrary, it got worse and worse.

A young man came to see me. He had witnessed the accident and, without my knowledge, he had regularly kept up on news of my condition. He told me that they were treating me incorrectly, and that he was going to take me to the best surgeon in Paris, and that these leg injuries were nothing to laugh at.

The next day, a large man came at nine in the morning. He came straight into my bedroom, and I asked him what he wanted.

"All right. Take the bandages off your legs. I'm taking your case at the request of M. Gustave de Bel…"

I obeyed, but I trembled because he scared me. He seemed very tough. He pressed on my knee to make me cry out. He looked at my red, swollen knee, which had only closed halfway.

"What imbecile has been taking care of you?" he said as he placed two fingers on either side of the cut.

I thought he was going to squeeze it. I took both his hands in mine. "Come on, you must have a child, right? What would you do for her? Can you not save this beautiful leg?"

He pressed a little. I began to cry.

"Cry, cry," he said. "It'll make you feel better."

The door of my bedroom opened, and I saw my mother in tears.

"Maman!" I said, forgetting the doctor, who hadn't forgotten me. Taking advantage of my distraction, he removed the partially healed, scarred flesh.

My heart skipped a beat. I threw myself back with a scream. I felt something warm run along my foot. He was given a towel, which became soaked with black blood. When I caught my breath, it was to cry. I retracted my leg, which I no longer wanted to entrust to this ass.

He laughed at my anger. "You're happy to hate me, eh? I didn't come here to make friends. I want to heal you. That wound was poorly closed. It would have sent you to the morgue's door. Now I have to see if the bone has anything wrong, and I have to cauterize you."

"Never!" I said. "You will not touch me at all. I'd rather die."

"Then I'll leave." And he crossed his arms.

"Come on," my mother said to me, "have a little courage!"

I was ashamed of my weakness, and I put my foot on his knee. He took a lancet, cut the flesh, and lightly scraped the bone.

Sweat beaded on my brow. My mother gripped my hand. With the other, I held the drapes so tightly that I made holes in it with my nails. He rubbed the infernal stone around the opening to cauterize the wound. I prayed for mercy.

He stopped and said, "That's enough for today. We can take it up again in two days. You're going to put a waxed cloth over this. You will place a wooden block under your knee to keep it raised. You'll take an alembic that will be given to you; you will fill it with ice, which will melt drop by drop onto your leg, day and night."

My mother led him out. She returned to me very pale.

Once the pain had subsided, I asked her how she knew my address and who told her I was hurt.

"On my block," she said, "there's a woman who has seats on the lower benches at the Hippodrome, Rosalie. One day she gave me the gift of two seats. I came to see this Céleste who is talked about so much but couldn't possibly be my daughter. When I recognized you, I nearly fainted. I wanted to hold you, but I didn't dare come see you backstage. I never wanted to return to see you do those awful races; I was too afraid. For two days, I heard news about you, but after six days, I didn't hear anything more. Rosalie told me they were saying that you must have cut your leg in the accident. So here I am. Do you want me to go?"

"Non, just the opposite."

What she said cut into my thigh like a steel blade. I felt chilled to the bone. I remained thoughtful. I consoled myself by saying that, if I had to submit to this operation, I would kill myself.

My mother moved nearby. I didn't dare ask her about her private life. She understood my discretion and told me she could give me all her time, as she lived absolutely alone.

&

I received a visit from my colleagues. Angèle, whose personality I'd never liked, was one of the more attentive visitors. I tried my best to get to know her, and I will never forget her. Everyone came to see me at first, but then I was left alone.

My giant of a surgeon sent word and came to see me a second time. I was massively afraid.

He patted my cheek and said, "Well, my child, the wounds are pink. You're saved. I caused you pain for your own good. What else would you want from me? There was no way to do anything less. The heat coming off the wounds was so great and the blood was so clogged by fear that I believed it was gangrene. You're out of danger. You've been very well-behaved. Try, if you can, not to continue in this line of work."

"Monsieur," I said, "how do I repay you for the care you've given me?"

"You have nothing to repay. I'm not a practicing

doctor anymore. It takes a situation like this for me to get involved. I'm too fat; I can't get up and down stairs easily anymore. Be sure that I never have to see you again. And if you value your limbs, which are going to cause you trouble, take care of yourself."

He left without telling me his name. I never knew it.

My mother also advised me to leave the Hippodrome.

⁂

B…, knowing I was unwell, had forgotten that he was refusing to talk to me. He engaged me to be at his side so I wouldn't end up in another job just as perilous. I promised him that I'd quit the Hippodrome at the end of the season if they didn't give me a raise.

I started to do laps around my bedroom, then I went downstairs. I walked with a sharp pain in my knee.

I took a coach to the Hippodrome. My role had been filled. They remembered me only to hurt me. This put me in such a fury that I demanded that they turn over my costumes and my horses for the next show. I'd been clearly told that I didn't have the strength to perform, but I didn't want to hear it.

When I climbed back into my chariot, which had been refitted for me, I felt a wave of emotion. The crowd applauded me. I lost my senses and leaped into the second lap.

This caused a new accident. The chariot behind me was up inside mine for a moment. Someone yelled, "Stop!" Angèle reined in her horse, and the chariot turned cleanly. One inch more and the shaft would have hit me between the shoulders. I hadn't seen the danger. I was calm, in step. When they told me what could have happened to me, I began to laugh. I thanked Angèle and said, "I'm going to end up killing myself in my chariot, like Hippolyte."

"Don't laugh," said Angèle. "I died of fright! You're not healed enough. You should rest for another two weeks."

I did, not so much because of my willpower but because I was forced. Boredom overtook me, and everything looked black.

I told my mother that if she wanted, I'd leave my life and go with her. As soon as I had a little money, we would go hide ourselves away in some corner of the city. She agreed.

※

The season was over. I asked for a meeting with my director to find out what his intentions were for me, if he wanted to hire me for two years and give me a raise.

He looked at me and said, "Why would I give you a raise? Aren't you still practicing *your business*? What are a few hundred francs more or less per year to you? I'm looking to cut everyone's pay. I have more women than I need. You should be happy if I keep you on at the same rate."

"This is the pay that I deserve for my work. I'll go, because next year, you'll be asking me to pay you money for the honor of working with you."

He didn't stop me. I went home hopeless.

My mother consoled me and told me, "Aren't they in a hurry? Maybe it's their awkwardness that makes them ingrates."

I didn't want to listen at all. I had two great sorrows

and an all-consuming worry. I had left my horses, for which I had a great passion, and I no longer had status. My anxieties were going to return.

I held back my tears, and I took a coach to go look after my affairs.

Up to the last minute, I had hoped that they were going to keep me on at the Hippodrome, but nothing. Not even a polite goodbye.

What could I do to console myself for this latest round of ingratitude? This is what I did: I swore never to go back to the Hippodrome as a horseback rider.

To snap myself out of it, I decided to run the world. I went to Lise's as soon as I could, then to Lagie's.

I had several times run into a short blond man with dark skin, a military type who swore and drank. He was witty, bad-tempered, eager to fight, and rarely polite. He was named Deligny. I disliked him so much that I never went somewhere without asking if he would be there in order to avoid him. He noticed that I didn't care for him and searched for ways to mock me.

So when he gave a dinner, I was invited to hide myself in the shadow of his presence. We fought all night. He boasted of never having been in love and of abusing women. They say that love often shows up holding hate by the hand. That's what happened.

He drank less in front of me, and he became almost friendly. This made him very happy, but it took a huge effort of will to quash the mockery.

❦

One day my mother told me, "You should set yourself up with a shop. I would take care of your household, which would make a position in society for you. I could stay nearby without being your responsibility."

This idea cheered me up. I gave my notice to my landlord. My mother looked for a boutique and found one, no. 2 rue Geoffrey-Marie. I rented rooms at no. 5, almost across the street.

While we were preparing to move, I received a letter from the Hague. It was from the baron, who had sent my fake sister my way. He had given up on any attempt at friendship with me because his service to the king had called him back to Holland. He told me in this letter that he had become very ill, and that my face kept coming to mind. My presence would heal him more than the help of the doctors.

Six months earlier or six months later, I would have sent him packing with this ridiculous sentiment. But it came at exactly the right time. I needed a distraction. The idea of taking a trip made me smile. A week in a foreign country seemed like excellent preparation for the commercial career that I was about to enter.

I didn't hesitate one second. I told my mother that I would leave that evening for Anvers, and go from there to the Hague. I would bring along my maid and be back in a week, maybe more.

My mother took me to the train station and cried hot tears on seeing me leave.

16.

Travelogue

Almost all the men behaved like gentlemen on the trip. However, there were many who excused themselves when they noticed a woman in the train car, saying "Let's go to another car. We can't smoke here."

Two particular young men were about to enter the car where I was seated when they closed the door to go look for seats elsewhere. After checking the entire train, they came back, having found no other seats. I saw on their faces that they were cursing me. I could have reassured them that a cigar wouldn't bother me at all since I myself smoked cigarettes. But it was more fun to tease them.

One of them, forgetting this little dispute over smoking, took a seat near me. He wanted to make up with me, if he could, by telling me a story. I said maybe yes, maybe no. He was put off and didn't say another word to me.

I wasn't very talkative, and I liked small talk even less. My companions spoke quietly together then arranged themselves in their corner to sleep. I wasn't sleepy, and I wanted them to keep me company. I had kept a surefire way to cheer them up in my pocket.

"If you want to smoke, messieurs," I said, "go ahead. It doesn't bother me. On the contrary, I like the smell of tobacco."

They all fumbled at the same time in their pockets and only thanked me after they'd cut off the ends of their cigars with their teeth. I was sure that after this, they would find me charming through the cloud of smoke that surrounded me. For certain people, smoking is more imperative than eating. I'd made them so happy that they made up for everything by being polite and paying attention to me. They escalated their kindness by bringing me sweetened water and cakes in the car, which I didn't want to put down.

At first, they were intrigued by me. Then, once they recognized me from the Hippodrome, they became excited and held nothing back. I reminded myself that this was how men are and that they must stay within bounds.

My maid snored louder than the locomotive, which we found hilarious. She kept falling onto her neighbor, who propped her up with his cane and greatcoat. She slept even as the train jolted, and we laughed at her.

It was horribly cold. Like everyone who has never traveled, I was in a tight-fitting half corset, as if I were going to a wedding. By the time we arrived at the station in the morning, I was ashen and flattened by fatigue.

I went to the hotel de la Poste in Brussels and slept for a few hours, which put me right. After breakfast, I took a tour of the city. It's basically Paris with fewer monuments and Parisians. All the streets going up and down annoyed me, and I didn't have time to stop over for very long. I had thought that Brussels had some kind of cachet. I came back to the station disillusioned.

I left for Anvers in a train that shook so hard the passengers knocked our foreheads against one another. Luckily the trip wasn't very long.

I arrived in Anvers all out of sorts. I asked where to find a steamboat with service to the Hague. I spoke to a tall man with chubby cheeks who asked me to repeat my question three times then in the end signed to me that he didn't understand. I cursed him to hell in French. He gave me a big wave.

An employee came to tell me that the steamboat wasn't running due to ice. They would be restarting service in a fortnight. The man made me grumpy, and I wanted to hit him. But since I was weak with fatigue and I wasn't as bold as Lola Montes, I took it in stride. I gave myself an air of importance and said that I was attending to some business that I could not share. It was necessary for me to leave at any price.

"Ma'am! There are many coaches, but you'll be miserable in one of those."

"That's none of your concern. Where are they?"

He pointed to the hotel Cheval Blanc.

I was given a room with two beds for myself and my dolt of a maid, whom I had to serve. After this, I wouldn't know how to give her orders anymore, and she might very well not know how to obey.

A fat woman came to set a match to the stove.

Imagine a coal fire in the middle of a room. The exhaust pipe of the stove was clogged. I spent the day with the window open and was soon doing polka steps to warm up, stomping my shoe leather on the floor. There was no other room available, and I couldn't leave because I was waiting for the coach. I asked to eat, and they brought me beer.

I reserved two outside seats in the coach. A third came with us, a gentleman—no exaggeration—as huge as half a barrel. I had to make myself small, or he would have crushed me. I carried half of his weight for two hours. At the first stop, I offered him the corner seat under the pretext of wanting to chat with my maid. This didn't rid us of him, and I began to regret this trip.

We had to change coaches ten times. We got out of one coach to take a sleigh that glided between cracks in the ice. We got into another sleigh, then a boat. This wasn't without peril and heightened anxiety. It has to be good business to travel this way, between snow and ice sleighs. It helped that we were only three travelers. Our companion seemed to be about thirty years old. He was wrapped in fur, and his scarf kept his face from being seen. What I did see seemed to be imprinted with great sadness. His eyes were red. But since the weather had given everyone red noses, I thought that it may have given him red eyelids too.

The barque we got onto was a kind of large raft that came to a point at the front, and it was bladed like a skate. We took on a new traveler. He had a coach exactly like the wagons that bring money from the bank. He disembarked from the coach, helped unhitch the horses, and carefully parked the coach on the ferry. He spoke Dutch with the sailors.

We moved forward and heard only the cracking of the ice. I was bored. I wanted to chat with my new companion. He was silently leaning over the front of his coach. Maybe he didn't know word of French. I let him be.

My maid was named Joséphine. She was dying of fear and cold. I myself was not very confident, but I put on a brave face to convince both of us. "Come on, Joséphine, be brave! You only die once. That carriage is having the same effect on me as emptying a beer too fast. The fish won't eat you."

"Madame, you're always laughing. I'm angry that I came."

The young man said in very good French, "Mademoiselle is right, it is a bier, but it's not empty."

I ran far enough away from the carriage to put some space between myself and it. "Not empty?" I said. "So we're traveling with the dead?"

"My father, mademoiselle," he said, removing his hat as if to honor those who were still mourning. His eyes were full of tears.

I was ashamed of how little decorum I'd had, of my levity. I wanted to apologize to him. Thinking that no one on the barque understood me, I'd said a thousand stupid things to my companion. I didn't dare move.

Now that I think about it, I do not understand why the dead are taken on trips.

I spoke quietly to Joséphine. The young man heard us, or guessed what I was saying. He came over to me and said, "This happens sometimes. I live in the Hague; my father died in Paris. His last wish was to be buried near his people. I obtained permission to bring him into the country. Don't be afraid. He was the best of men. He could only bring good luck."

Just then, I heard harsh words. Without understanding the language, I could easily see that our sailors were swearing. They took the boathooks and worked to push back the enormous ice floes that had joined together and closed off our passage.

The young man was in a hurry and had paid four times the usual price for a ticket. We had taken this large ferry, although it was turning out to be a mistake. The company was no fun, and neither was the situation. I hid my head in my hands and fervently prayed to God. When I was done, I saw many men at the port as we approached with difficulty.

Once on land, Joséphine and I got into a waiting coach. Two horses were hitched to the young man's coach, and he walked at its head with much dignity.

We crossed the town, which was, I think, Rotterdam. I only saw the mileposts, the channels, and the gates. The countryside was flooded, and the water that covered the fields was frozen. Here and there, children skated.

When we were several miles yet from the Hague, the country came to life. The fields were covered with skaters. The women wore round baskets on their heads and held sweaters in their hands as they glided like swallows that shear the earth so easily, effortlessly, which amazed me for the rest of the ride. They were going from one town to another to visit, to meet, to chat, then to move on. It was sweet. I was enchanted, and I wanted to try it.

We stopped at an inn. I bought skates and gave it a try. At my first attempt, I fell spreadeagle. On my second, the same. The only thing I learned was that you never fall forward. I was stubborn, but the ice was hard, and I had to give up. When I had to sit in the coach again, I was sorry I hadn't stopped skating sooner.

Finally we arrived in the Hague. I was staying at the hotel de l'Europe. I had asked for the best in the city, and this is where I was sent. All the bedrooms had a small stove, which made me happy.

The Hague is a very dour city. Solo French travelers are received coldly when they're anything less than sixty years old. The clerks at the hotel looked at me, they hesitated. I noticed the moment when they were about to welcome me. I said, "Give me whatever you've got. I'm not choosy. I'll be leaving in ten days."

I was shown to a very nice room on the first floor. Another plainer room opened off of it. Each had its little stove polished like a pair of boots. I made those stoves glow red.

I wrote a note to my friend, who was feeling better. He was on duty and could only see me for a minute that evening, yet many precautions still needed to be taken.

He came with his head on a swivel like a man being followed. He spoke to me quietly and begged me to remain incognito. The idea of passing myself off as a noble foreigner made me smile.

❦

The next day, I went to see the Scheveningen district. Coming to the beach, I walked in fine, yellow sand as near as possible to the sea. While my feet were in the sand, it became misty. My maid and I were alone, so I lifted my skirt enough to keep it from getting dirty. I was wearing blue-buttoned boots that were a little tight, along with silk stockings. This was probably not the fashion here.

Joséphine began to yell, "Oh my God, madame!"

I thought something was climbing up my legs. I lifted my skirts up a little more. Not seeing anything on the ground, I put them back down. Then I saw behind me maybe two hundred men dressed all alike: pants and yellowish jackets, hats with large brims, like at our forts at la Halle. Many were bent over and looking at—my stockings, surely.

I lowered my dress all the way. I didn't dare move. I had heard it said that sailors abducted women and took them onto boats, and after having their way with them, they tossed them into the sea. Luckily a Dutchman with a golden badge appeared. This emboldened me.

The men who had made me so afraid moved aside to let us pass. I was scared of a tragic end! *If they want to take me,* I said to myself, *I'll throw myself into the sea.*

One of them waved to me. I came to my senses and laughed. These were oystermen.

The next day was a lovely day on the ice. The sun was a pale disk, but it sparkled.

The concierge recommended that I visit the park. I put on a black velvet dress, a matching cape, a white beaded hat with roses on it, and a veil, more to keep my nose from turning red than to hide myself. This park was wonderful. There were deer that were almost tame.

I saw a tall, blonde lady in front of me with her hair undone, in the English style. Some people walked next to her, and passersby saluted her respectfully. She smiled. She looked at me, spoke to a lady near her, and continued on her way. I heard everyone saying, "The queen!" I could only assume this was the woman I'd crossed paths with.

I saw my baron come out of an alley on lovely gray horse. I was about to ask him if this lady was indeed the queen, but when he saw me, he turned abruptly. I think that, if he hadn't had obstacles in his way, he'd still be running.

I went back to the hotel to dine.

The baron came to see me for one minute and told me that during my walk that morning, I had unknowingly fallen into the midst of the entire court. I understood why he'd taken off—he was a chamberlain. I didn't mean to commit an indiscretion; everyone is a chamberlain in this country.

He sent me to see a show. They were performing *The Count of Ory* and *Figaro*. The space was unique, in that there were no boxes in this theater. A gallery separated most of the seats for the chamberlains, ladies, and the king. The most prominent people of the town were in the orchestra seats. I pouted when they showed me my seats.

My white hat caught the eye of many young men seated in the balcony. They wanted to know whose face was under this hat. Many came to the door of the orchestra seats. I had entered in majestic fashion, and I maintained a dignified air.

Alas! I had not counted on the embarrassment of my fame. During the intermission, two curious men came to sit almost across from me.

"It's not possible," said one.

"Come on, then," said the other.

"I'm sure," answered the first. "I know her. I saw her often enough at the Hippodrome. You'll see."

The two of them left but came back with reinforcements. This new man took me in with a nasty squint.

"You're wrong," said the newcomer.

"No, no," said the rat, "I definitely recognize her. She's a little pockmarked. That's definitely her. I bet the baron could tell us one way or the other."

Luckily the curtain went up and they didn't dare turn back around. I had been very vexed. Now I had a desire to laugh that choked me.

Maestro Basile came onstage. I could release my quiet hilarity as I wished. They made such funny faces, and I looked at them with such a grand air of indignation when they called me Mogador that I didn't dare turn my head. I was on the edge of a very embarrassing exit.

The performance wasn't quite finished when I left my seat. I hoped to make it all the way to my hotel unbothered. I lingered at the door, but the men had left their seats at the same time as me, and they were wandering in the hallway.

I saw the baron at the door. He turned his back to me, signaling that I was to get into an open coach at the bottom of the stairs. A man pushed me, and I heard someone speaking to the coachman, but I didn't understand him. We left in the middle of a train of coaches. We drove for a long time, and I began to worry, because I should have reached the hotel in half an hour.

I wanted to speak to the coachman, but he didn't understand French. He doubled his speed. I saw trees, the river. I understood that I was lost. He was leading me into the woods. I got it—he thought I was rich. They were going to rob me and kill me. I begged my maid's forgiveness for having put her in danger for days. I didn't know if it was the road or fear that wore down my nerves, but I began to cry. My maid cried along in another key. It was earsplitting.

The carriage stopped. I recognized the hotel.

"Idiot!" I said as I got out. He'd been lost.

"No," said the baron, who was waiting at the door. "I ordered him to take a long detour; otherwise, you'd have been followed. I don't want to them to know where you're staying. Good evening, until tomorrow. Don't go out, and don't go to the window."

"So I'm in prison, then?"

"What I'm telling you is in your best interest. One of our compatriots from the Hippodrome, Mlle. Hermance, was sent back to France because everyone was too preoccupied with her."

"There's not a lot of hospitality in this country. I'll leave tomorrow."

"No, stay a few more days. The roads are a mess."

Since I was staying alone, I found one distraction: stoking my stove, opening the window so as not to roast, then getting into bed and sleeping. Sleep! Was it even possible? My maid snored like a drumroll.

⁂

I got up early and looked for something to keep me busy. The search was in vain, and I spent four hours yawning. I was loosening up my clothes to take them off when I heard voices chatting as they came up the stairs.

I stood there with my arms in the air. They said my name. I thought the baron had sent me a group of visitors, that he'd sent his friends, so I went to open the door. I saw five young men, but not the baron. I quickly slammed it shut, but it was too late. They'd seen me. I listened at the door while they talked about me.

One said, "I knew that she had to be staying here."

The door next to mine opened onto a salon where these men had come to dine. They knocked on the wall between the rooms and sang songs about me, or songs that they improvised. They got nasty.

I didn't move, and I wouldn't answer them for anything in the world. It was, however, very funny.

At eight o'clock that evening, someone knocked on my door. I refused to open up since I didn't recognize it as the voice of my friend. A short note was passed under the door:

> *I didn't dare come see you. Your hotel has been invaded. Go out at ten o'clock. I'll wait for you at the corner of the square and café Anglais.*

The hour came. I wrapped myself up like a spy, and Joséphine and I slid along the walls like two shadows. The city at this hour was as quiet and bleak as a cemetery.

We moved slowly, as there was so much black ice. Joséphine slipped and went down in a heap. Luckily I was the only one around to see her; otherwise, I'd have had a heart attack. I began to laugh so hard I had to lean against the wall.

A sentry was walking silently nearby. She stopped to listen and called out, "Who's there?" I didn't know what to answer. It seemed impossible to not laugh.

"Oh, madame!" said Joséphine. "It's not nice to laugh at others. It's not exactly a good time, sitting here on the sidewalk."

I didn't dare take another step. The sentry called out again, and I answered, "It's us!"

It seemed this wasn't sufficient. Luckily the baron had noticed that I was late. He appeared in front of us and said something to this small-time sentry. He didn't even make fun of us, which he surely could have done.

"It's you!" I said. "I'm so glad, because we can't go any farther."

"Why are you laughing so hard then?"

"Joséphine won't move without being shod for the ice."

"You have to change hotels tomorrow. They were already asking who the foreign woman is that they've seen on the promenade, and now they know who you are. Since there's a dearth of charming women like you here, when one comes to town, it's an event. Young men lose their minds."

"My dear, your country is boring. I'm not changing hotels. I'll leave tomorrow. It's not your fault. I'm glad to go, and it won't cause you any more grief. Hire me a coach."

He tried to make me stay, but my resolve was set and my patience had reached its end.

The journey back was as troublesome as the journey there, and I saw the wharf of Paris with the joy of an exile.

17.

The Death of Marie

My mother had arranged everything for the move. Our boutique was ready.

I had saved a little money, but it wasn't enough. I sold my jewelry, my cashmere. I paid all my little debts, as I wanted a clean break with all the shopkeepers who hang on you and profit from your position as a courtesan, from your lack of knowledge, as they sell things to you.

I didn't want to become tame and virtuous, but I did want to leave this service at the pleasure of others. I wanted to laugh only when I wanted to laugh and to make myself happy. I wanted to live frugally, only according to my need if necessary. I wanted to be happy whatever came my way.

I remembered the Sundays of my childhood. They

may not have been overly joyous, but they were little celebrations. I remembered the dress from my first communion, which I wore until the waist came up to my armpits. I thought it was lovely because I didn't have another dress to wear.

I began looking at the sky four days in advance to see if it would rain. That's not the kind of thing the gadabouts of the world do. The abuse of pleasure erodes vivacity and intelligence. You became insensate to everything, especially simple things. Naïve joy, which is the best kind, is impossible. You see too much. What is Sunday for rich people? A boring day.

These days, the sightseers amuse themselves. It's better not to do as they do. They go to the countryside and seek out some secluded spot, not so much out of an enthusiasm for nature as out of disdain for the city in its Sunday best and the suburbs in its cups.

Nevertheless, my lovely ladies and good gentlemen, these sightseers, whom you mock, are elated by a little fresh air, and their elation is often better than yours. Observe the sightseers who return Sunday evening. They went out into the countryside to pick up a currant branch or a bouquet of wild flowers. They're tired and dusty, but they had enough fun to last a week.

I compare these pleasures of my childhood to the pleasures of this gilded youth, in the middle of which I was now living, and I found the former much more preferable. What did they think was fun, all these young people? They thought they were being original in following Anglomania and Regency traditions. The most inventive rode tall, skinny horses. They dressed as servants. They galloped off, sometimes to the forest in Boulogne, sometimes to Champs-de-Mars. They fell from the saddle two or three times, they lost money, they dined every day at restaurants, and gambled half the night with their mistresses. They went to the ball with their circle of friends, and in all this, they couldn't find a way to have actual fun for more than an hour. I don't even want to hear about a world where, to be respectable, you have to be thin and jaundiced. These are the people who say that they were given their lives to end them.

I saw these two ways of life. The lives of the hikers seemed to me a lot more fun, and I made a plan to rejoin them.

My boutique was very pretty. My mother had set it up marvelously, but we couldn't put together five hundred francs from what we had left over. My mother took on good workers, and the openings of fashion shops were fixed at *twenty* per month. We were at *nine*.

The apartment that I rented was across the street on the second floor, overlooking the courtyard. I happily arranged my own furniture. I'd sent Joséphine away. She didn't sleep if she thought she could steal from me. So I hired a girl from Nantes named Marie. She was small, with cat-gray eyes and a large nose. She seemed rather dim, and it wasn't an act. I'd been told good things about her, that she was trustworthy.

At the time, I had a little white dog with black spots which I'd raised from a puppy. Blanchette was happy and friendly, and I held her all the time. I was afraid to lose her to illness, because she had a chronic cough. An employee at the shop advised me to give her a powder that was advertised all over Paris as preventing illness. I asked her to bring me some, and the next day I gave my little dog the designated dosage. I told Marie to shut the dog in the kitchen.

An hour later, I heard cries, like those of a baby. I was stopped cold in my bedroom. I thought something had happened to the neighbor. Soon enough, the crying stopped, but it was replaced by screams and moans.

The door to the kitchen was open. I heard Marie trying to keep the dog from escaping. The poor beast ran between her legs and collapsed at my bedroom door. Then I heard groaning, so I opened the door and saw my poor Blanchette lying at the threshold. White foam was coming out of her mouth, and her eyes rolled back in her head. She wagged her tail feebly when she saw me and wanted to get up and come to me. But standing pained her so much, she fell back down. She offered her paws one last time and fell dead at my feet, her tongue on my hand.

This caused me true grief. Maybe it's embarrassing to cry for a dog, but I shed tears. I had poisoned this poor beast with too strong a dose.

I had always been superstitious. The death of my dog was not only devastating, it seemed like a bad omen. I no longer liked my apartment. I was too sad.

❧

We had several employees at the shop. One missed work one day, so my mother asked me to go to the home of the woman who had recommended her. Maman said that she lived on rue Coquenard. I wore a shawl, a hat, a veil, and I went via fauborg Montmartre.

I walked slowly. Something invisible seemed to be pulling me from behind. I turned around to see if someone was there. Twice I wanted to turn back. But at last I came to the corner, where I heard a deafening scream, then more voices yelling, and I saw everyone running. I stepped forward, and a crowd of people gathered around something on the ground.

I ran up and pushed people aside with both hands. They had picked up a woman off the street. I let out a terrible cry. The shop girl offered me her hand, and I took it. It gripped mine. Her blonde hair was undone and hid part of her face. Her beautiful eyes, which had been so brilliant, dulled like frost beneath my breath.

"Goodbye," she murmured. She squeezed my hand harder.

"Marie!" I cried, kissing her. "Marie! Come back! My God, how awful. She's not dead, is she? We can revive her?"

An elderly man touched his forehead, took off his hat, and said, "It's all over." I felt my heart rip open and release a torrent of tears.

She was taken back up to her rented furnished room. I followed this sad cortege. She had left only a letter and asked that it be delivered to the address written on it without being opened. I could see that this was the grief that had pushed her out the window.

She was laid out on her small bed. A doctor said she had broken her spine and severed the arteries to her heart. Death must have been instantaneous. Her eyes were still open, her cheeks were drawn, and she was thin.

I knew who she'd addressed this letter to, and I promised myself I'd go see him. In the meantime, I hastily sent the letter with a messenger.

There were a lot of people packed into Marie's room. They asked me if I knew the parents of this poor dead girl. I said no. They asked the woman who rented to her how long she had lived there.

"It was a little more than two months. I evicted her because I found out she was registered with the police as a prostitute. I have a little girl, so I couldn't let her stay."

"Did she have friends? Did anyone from outside come see her?"

"Non, monsieur, she never received anyone at my place. I thought she was sick all the time."

They wrote down all the details.

I sent along a dress for her to be buried in, plus a cape and a bonnet. I didn't have the courage to assist with getting her ready, but I suggested they arrange her hair nicely. She had always taken such care with it. I recalled one day she had said to me, "I wouldn't die at a hospital for anything in the world for fear that they would cut my hair."

Her lover, I told myself, would want to bury her. I wanted to find him.

I went back home deflated. Everyone was distraught by the news. It was good that they didn't know her well; it was a sad story.

Her lover lived on rue Racine. I took a coach because I didn't have the strength to walk. It was four o'clock when I arrived at the door of his building. I went to the concierge, and the first thing I saw on the table was the letter from Marie. Fuck him. I asked if the concierge knew where the gentleman was, saying that it was absolutely necessary that I speak with him.

The porter didn't seem at all disposed to go look, but his wife, who was nicer, told me that he was at the bar next door. She said I only had to ask for him.

I spoke to a little boy in the bar, and they called for the man in the billiard room.

"Wait at my place," the man said via the messenger.

"I'm finishing up."

I asked the boy to tell the man to hurry because I had something important to tell him, and I was going to wait at the porter's next door.

"He said he wouldn't leave early for all the money in the world!" the boy reported.

I waited next door for an hour. At last he came in, slovenly and ashen. He was an older student but still young, handsome enough for his type, but as bad a specimen as it's possible to be.

"It's you," he said when he recognized me. "Why didn't you come into the bar? You could have had absinthe with us. I won my game."

"Don't laugh, my friend. I bring you sad news. Read this letter." I pointed to the letter from Marie on the table.

"Again!" he said. "If this is what you came for, you could have stayed home. I guess I never threw that away." He put his hands on his forehead in exasperation. "I told her not to write to me. I don't want to read her letters." He was about to rip it up.

I stopped his hands. "Read this," I said. "It's the last letter that you'll receive."

"She's told me that a hundred times. I have ten upstairs that I've never opened."

"You're wrong. You've maybe avoided a great misfortune. This is definitely the last of them. She's dead."

"Dead!" He looked at me.

"Oui, dead. She threw herself out the window and left only this letter for you."

He took his key, asked the porter if there was a fire in his room, and took me upstairs. On entering his apartment, he took off his cap, tossed back his hair, and opened the letter. It was eight or ten pages. He lit a candle and read. He shook his head, but he didn't shed a tear.

Poor Marie! She'd loved this man for years. She'd killed herself for him.

At last he said, "It's an atrocity, but it can't be helped now. I can't do anything. But in the end it's the best thing that could have happened to her. I've had another mistress for a year, whom I love very much. I kept her a secret for a while, but Marie followed me and discovered everything. I didn't have anything more to get from Marie, and I resolved to end it. I told her that I didn't love her anymore, that I was keeping my other mistress because she calmed me down. Then there were the tears, those irritating sobs. She became almost feverish. One evening, she came with the intent to kill me. She had a knife! I was about to go my mistress's, so I shut Marie in an empty bedroom next door to give her anger time to blow over. She made such a racket that I spent the night elsewhere."

"You weren't afraid of her despair?"

"No. After I'd left, she was told that if she came again and made a ruckus in the house, they'd find a policeman to arrest her."

"That's awful. You have no heart."

"I do in fact have a heart, but I couldn't stand Marie. You should have seen her. I'd never known torture like that, to have someone beside you who torments you because of a love you don't share. Only a saint could bear it. I only have one regret, and that's that I didn't feel for her what I felt for another. But I can't help that. If she only wanted my friendship, I would have offered it, because she was a nice girl. I'm sorry now for having been so harsh with her, but she was the one who had no heart. I was straight with her, but she kept coming back anyway."

"Because she adored you. You were her weakness. It's cruel of you to accuse her of having no heart. Don't you think she didn't have to kill herself at her age?"

He reread the letter without any more emotion than the first time. He had a heart of stone. But marble girls have not yet been invented.

Someone knocked on the door. He had taken his key out of the lock. "Who is it?" he asked.

"Moi!" said a woman's voice.

He set aside the letter and opened the door. A short brunette came in, nose in the air.

"Wait," she said, looking at me, "you know Mogador? That's why I was told not to come up." And she made as if to go. He went to hold her back.

I knew that if poor Marie had found herself in front of this snob's daggers, she would have seen this nastiness. I picked up the letter so this woman wouldn't see it. I knew that she would use this scene to get her vengeance on Marie.

She said to him, "Is Marie still sending people to look for you? Go, my dear, it's all the same to me. It's not me who's running after you. I don't need you. You know that I'm not jealous."

This pissed me off. I got up to give her my seat and said that Marie hadn't sent me to look for her lover. She could keep him without sharing. I had come to ask him to bury her and to take him to her last resting place.

"You see?" he said, blocking her exit.

I left without his even saying thank you. I began to see his point. If it was Marie's destiny to be unable to free herself from this man, dying was the easiest way to do it.

In my haste, I had accidentally brought along the letter from this poor child. I figured I'd give it back to him the next day because I was sure he'd come to my place. Here are some excerpts:

Marie's the Shop Girl's Letter

At least read this letter to the end. Don't laugh; I've told you this often enough. It's because I always hoped that I would touch your heart, that you would pity me.

My crime is that I love you too much. Forgive me. I'm going to pay dearly for it. I've never been brave when it comes to letting you go. You ignored me when I so hard despite the coldness that you showed me. I returned and asked your forgiveness for wrongs I had done to you. I threw myself at your feet and asked for your mercy. I wanted to leave you if you no longer loved me. You hunted me! I sent you my soul and my tears in letters that you burned without response, or that your mistress sent back with an insult in her handwriting.

My despair ignites your love for her, but she doesn't love you. She loves another. But it's so much fun to torture my heart that, in order to make me suffer, she splits her time between the other man and you.

You'll be sorry, and not only because you love her. When I'm not around anymore, she'll leave you. Maybe then you'll think of me. You'll reread this letter that I'm begging you to keep, and to make it up to my departed soul for the way you've treated my heart and body, you will do what I advise. Leave the Latin Quarter and return to Bretagne, where your mother still waits for you. I've seen you receive letters from her. She is heartbroken by your leaving. She begs you to come back to the countryside. You don't even answer her.

You've been in Paris fifteen years; this life of billiards and bars has spoiled your habits and withered your face. I thought you were the most handsome man in the world because I loved you like a fool. But a love this good—you'll never find it again. You'd recognize it and then flee from it.

Leave while there's still time. If you wait much longer, maybe you'll only see the tomb of your mother, sainted woman, who only has you. If she saw into the depths of my heart, she would love me because of the love I have for you.

If you want me to remain by your side, I would make myself so small that you wouldn't even notice me. If you held me in your hand, I would be purified through the strength of my devotion from the darkness where I'd fallen.

All of my life force clings to the memory of hope. I love you, I still love you! You are the first and last love of my life. The Creator made me lazy, but I would have found boundless energy if you had said to me, "Perform a miracle and I will love you!"

My mind is on fire. All right, it's impossible, it must end. I tried everything; however, I can't leave you. The idea that you would read this letter stops me. For two months, I've suffered a thousand deaths. If I could drag myself there, I would die near you, on your doorstep. I would see you one last time. I would write to you with my last breath.

If I had money to buy coal, I would tell you if death was as hard to bear as your leaving, but I have nothing. I have only my window and the river. I can't get there. I took a knife and many times raised it to my breast, but I'm afraid of the cold blade, cutting…

My God, if you forgive me, let me die right away. I repent. I've begged you for two days. I'm going to forget you at the last moment.

My friend, I forgive you.

Soon, at this windowsill, I am going to kneel, join my hands, and bow forward. I will say, "My God, forgive me! My God, receive me with mercy! Let me die!"

Marie

This last prayer was granted, because she only released one breath, and then she was dead.

Back at home, I hid this letter and how I'd come to have it.

The next day, I didn't leave the house. I waited for her lover. I hadn't heard any news by four o'clock, but I thought that she must have been taken to rue Coquenard by then. I went there, but there was no one to see!

Marie's body had been removed from her apartment at two o'clock. The charity that had been given notice had provided its carriage for the indigent. No one accompanied her body.

Even dead, all creatures inspire respect. Passersby saluted her along the way to her final resting place.

I was told that reading Werther caused suicides. I read him, but at the time I was too happy or too ignorant to understand him. Reading him didn't even make me melancholy. But Marie was firmly lodged in my memory. I realized that nothing ends, even in the stillness of death. Every night, I see her in a dream. She speaks to me, and she always tells me the same thing.

18.

An Act of Despair

We began, my mother and me, our grand commercial operation. The shop was open. We'd had practice. All the women I had known came to my place to make their purchases.

However, we were not on the road to riches for the simple reason that these women bought on credit. I couldn't bring myself to refuse them. My mother made me understand that we couldn't do business this way, and she put herself in charge of refusing credit accounts.

❧

I don't know who was lying in wait for me, but I must have had a hidden enemy, because a rotten turn of events came my way.

My apartment was between two hallways. There was an antechamber, a salon and bedroom on the left, and a small room for a servant across the way. In the corner to the right was the door to the hallway that led into the kitchen, and across from this the pantry.

One morning, about eight or nine o'clock, someone rang. I had a huge headache, so I didn't get up. I told my maid Marie, who went to open the door. "I don't want to see anyone. Have them go down to the shop."

"Mademoiselle Céleste!"

"She's not here," said Marie. "If you'd like to see her mother, she is in the shop—"

"Non," said the voice, "I want to bring her in. She's made me chase after her for a long time. I know that she's here and that she's hiding. There's been a complaint brought against her, and I've been ordered to bring her in no matter where I find her."

My headache disappeared. I was sitting on my bed and holding my breath so I could hear Marie's response. I looked right, left—where could I escape if she said that I was there? I only saw the window.

"I don't know what you want me to say," answered this girl in a shaky voice. "If madame were here, I would have told you."

"Tell her that if she doesn't get herself to the station tomorrow before noon, I'm going to send around a policeman."

The door closed.

I hid my face in my hands. I was ashamed in front of this girl when she came back into my room. She was truly ashen.

"I don't know anything about it," I said. "He's mistaken. If I had been dressed, I would have come out. He'll come back, and you'll let him in. Don't speak of this to anyone; they'll jump to conclusions."

She promised to stay mum. I gave her permission to leave me; I needed to be alone. I squeezed my head in my hands. What was going to become of me? I couldn't save myself. I had put the little money I had into the shop. Everything for nothing…I fell back into fear and depression.

I could no longer go downstairs without risking being arrested and maybe sentenced to a month. I had to avoid the summons that had been issued. What were they saying in the neighborhood? Everyone knows this story; I'm not going to rehash it. For now and forever, I can do nothing to avoid it.

I thought of Marie. The next day was Sunday; they couldn't arrest me then because the offices were closed. My maid would be gone all day, and my mother wouldn't open the shop. I would be all alone—all alone. I was saved.

I took out some paper and spent my evening writing. At eleven o'clock, my mother came to wish me a good night.

"I thought you'd be asleep! You're writing to the suppliers?"

"Oui."

It didn't even cross my mind to hug her. I knew that she was seeing Vincent again. She'd hidden him from me, but I'd heard about it. The first young girl who'd said something had painted me a portrait that I knew all too well. Since my mother had forbidden her from telling me that she had a gentleman visitor, she didn't have any other convincing reason to come up to my room and tell me. She even told me that often, when I went downstairs, M. Vincent left by a back door that opened onto rue de la Boule-Rouge. This made me so angry I couldn't bear it. I found all my rage toward him buried in my heart, along with all of my coolness toward my mother.

Once I was alone again, I put everything in order. I tucked away some letters to my friends, and I went to bed almost happy with my little act.

※

I woke up the next morning. Toward ten o'clock, it began to rain so fine that looked like fog. I called for Marie.

"Come," I said to her, "get dressed and go for a walk. It's your day off."

"Oh, the weather is too awful," she said. "I only have my childhood friend to visit. I'll go to her house next week."

I hadn't accounted for this. I'd told my mother that I'd be dining elsewhere because my servant was out. I had told Maman to spend the day with friends. I didn't have to beg; M. Vincent was waiting.

This wouldn't do. It was absolutely necessary that Marie leave. I picked up a scrap of white paper under an envelope with a name written on it.

"I need you to take this to avenue Saint-Cloud," I said to Marie. I knew that her friend was on the Champs-Elysées. She would take advantage of this fact to go see her, and she would stay there long enough for me to execute my plan. I gave her my errand with orders to leave immediately. I called to her in the stairway to tell her I was going out and that she could stay at her friend's until one o'clock.

My door closed. I was alone, free. I felt true joy.

I went into Marie's bedroom and gathered all her things, which I took into my room. I put white linens on her little iron bed. I went to the kitchen and looked beneath the stove. There weren't any pieces of coal there, and my heart broke when I saw the basket for my little dog. That house had no good luck.

At the time, we all wore long, lightweight jackets. I had one in black silk, and I put it on. I went downstairs, trembling at the thought of meeting someone who would make me a minute late for my plan.

The pavement glistened, the sky was dark, the shops were closed. I had a moment of worry, but I exhaled when I saw that the pottery shop was open. I bought two clay pots of coal, which I took upstairs to my place, hiding them under my coat as if I were carrying a treasure. I returned to the coal box.

I lit the two stoves in Marie's room, and I shut myself in there, stopping up the windows and smallest cracks. I heard the crackling of the coal as it lit the room and seemed to say, "Despise yourself! Say your prayers." I even plugged the hole in the lock.

I sat on the bed. I asked forgiveness from God and from all those to whom I would cause pain. I waited, calm, as if I were sure of divine mercy. I fell asleep.

The brazier was behind my head. I had thought it was a good idea to hang a diaphanous cloth above me, and I hadn't thought about the fact that it would draw down when I breathed in. This was death. If I breathed deeply, I would no longer suffer.

I'm not going to die, I said to myself. *Tomorrow I'll be arrested.*

Maybe I didn't use enough coal.

I got up. I felt my body right itself despite feeling

off-kilter. I leaned on the bed with a feeling of joy. I got on my knees to restart the coal. The blue flame drew me in. I sat there in ecstasy, eyes fixed, mouth agape. I felt myself sway like the clapper in a bell. I was afraid of falling headfirst into the fire, so I dragged myself back.

At this movement, a band of iron wrapped around my head. The fire seemed to be in my chest. I placed my hands on myself to quiet the searing pains. My vision clouded over. I wanted to cry out, but my tongue and throat were swollen. I got up by sheer force of will and put both hands on a table. I looked at myself in a small mirror.

Horrors! My head was swollen, the veins in my forehead stood out, the arteries in my bare neck were like ropes, my lips were blue, and my hair was standing on end.

I sank to the floor and crawled. I could no longer see. Finally I could feel the door. I stood up, only to fall in a heap again. I had endured everything there is to endure in order to die. Nothing I write can portray this agony. It is particularly frightening for anxious people who thrash about in the end and try to save themselves.

When I came to, I was on my bed. My room was full of people. Two men were rubbing my arms, two others my legs—so hard I thought I'd been burned. I looked around through half-open eyes. The ache in my head made me think that I was out of my mind and that everything I was seeing was only shadows. The pain was too great for me to doubt it for long.

"She's saved," said the hairdresser who had the

boutique next to ours. She'd been one of the first to arrive and had carried me to safety.

"Saved! From what?" I asked.

My mother was next to my bed.

Everything came back to me, back to the threats from the police…

I began to weep and argue. I wanted to start over. I berated everyone for coming to help me. The two doctors declared that I was delirious and that I must not be out of someone's sight for a minute. My mother was wise enough to say that her presence was bothering me, so she left. Vincent was surely waiting for her. It was Marie who watched over me.

"How was I rescued?" I asked her, stunned to be alive after having gone through so much.

"Without me, madame, you'd be a goner. You gave me the day off, but it was so awful outside that I took the omnibus to deliver that letter and return instead of walking. I didn't find anyone at home where you sent me, so I came back to tell you. I didn't see you in your room, so I thought you'd gone out. I was in the kitchen when I saw so much smoke that I thought there must be a fire. I wanted to go into my room, but something was holding the door closed. You had fallen behind it. I didn't dare push because your face was against the opening. I thought you were dead, so I called for help. You were put on your bed, and you laid there three hours with no signs of life. The fire had taken the little bedroom. The floor in there is completely burned.

"The doctor said that you had fallen with your head facing the gap around the door, which gave you a tiny stream of clean air. Without that, you'd be gone."

"And I would have been glad!"

"Oh, madame, don't say things like that."

"My poor Marie, what you don't know. The man who came the other day will return, and then—"

"Don't torture yourself, madame. If he returns, I'll tell him that if he has to bring someone in to arrest me—me. And then no one else will come up here. If he saw you like this, he wouldn't have the heart to trouble you. Come on, madame, recover quickly and never have any more awful ideas like that. I haven't worked for you very long, but I like you very much."

She really did watch me day and night.

I begged all those around me to keep this adventure quiet. When one tries something like this, there's no need to say anything out of fear of ridicule.

I healed very slowly. But I did go down to the shop at the end of some days, despite the massive headaches, the vomiting, and a bothersome cough that tore at my chest.

19.

THE RETURN OF LISE

EVERYTHING WAS GOING FROM BAD to worse! The women that I'd refused to extend credit to never came back to the shop. The bills came due, and we didn't have the first sou put aside. The merchandise had been sold, and we had to pay for it. The vendors were going to come after me, snatch me up. I cried every day about not having killed myself.

If my maid, who watched over me with the loyalty of a poodle, hadn't kept such close a close eye on me, I would have done it again. I was depressed, ill. I let myself go and hoped for the end.

I sometimes went over to Lise's, but she was in Italy. The only person who would keep me company in my despair was Deligny.

When I had left for Holland, my feelings toward

him were still very bittersweet. That trip had been a way to break up with Deligny and the circle he traveled in. He was one of the flashiest of all of them. I already mentioned, I think, that he held himself with a military bearing and that he was a fighter, and for this he was mocked by all the women. He had a friend, Médème, who was pale, blond, and thin, and he followed Deligny's lead. It was all about who drank more, had more fights, changed mistresses most often. With this kind of personality, you'd think I wouldn't have held onto such a sharp and lasting memory. I never thought I'd see Médème again. I was therefore quite surprised when he came to visit me.

I was in such a state of mind that he did something extraordinary to get me to want to live. Deligny couldn't have performed this miracle, but Médème was exuberant and funny, and my life was so sad, so isolated, that I gladly made room for him. His visits were a distraction from my worries.

Our first meeting was short; we talked about this and that. He gave in to me on everything. It was almost like achieving a victory over his willful nature.

We spent some evenings together. I forbade him from getting drunk or swearing. His friends teased him for it. I had asked him not to at first, and then I forbade it. He obeyed me—grumblingly, but he obeyed. I found pleasure in winning this fight.

He had a good heart, but the wildest ideas in the world. He was from M…. His father had a large enough fortune, worth fifteen or twenty thousand livres, but he had four children and could only give his son a modest allowance, which was absorbed by his restaurant-based life.

Médème did everything he could to help me out, but he didn't lend me all that much. I didn't judge him for it. I could have abused his generosity. He signed checks for my unpaid bills. He had foolishly come to love me. I only used my influence over him to make him abandon that life full of people richer than he was. They would only cause his downfall.

He was a good painter. I got him to live and work among artists by renting a studio on avenue Frichot. I often heard people talk about Th. Rousseau, who advised Médème that, if he wanted to put in the work, he had the talent.

One day, I saw a woman stopped across from my window. She passed by all day long, which wasn't all that surprising on this street. Nevertheless, I let out a little, "Ah!" when I saw her.

"You know her?" said my mother.

"Oui," I said, and I got up.

I opened the door to see her better. She walked by without seeing me, crossed the street, and entered no. 7, across the way. A little later, the front window opened, and I saw a large woman known as Fond. This Fond was one of those former beauties who, after having wasted their own lives without thinking of the future, sold the youth and beauty of others. They loomed large in those women's lives, so much so that anyone who fell into their clutches had only the hospital or the river as prospects when they were let go. This woman Fond hid her odious business under the name Table d'Hote.

I went inside the shop at no. 7, wondering the whole

time, *Where have I seen that face?*

Just then a shopgirl came to ask me, "Would you be so kind as try on two or three hats, up there, on the first floor?"

I wanted to send my mother to do it, but curiosity got the best of me, and I went myself. It was, I think, curiosity that made me obey this request.

I was brought into a small, red salon, plainly decorated. The small woman I'd seen in the street came in and took off her hat.

"Have you tried on the pink? I quite like it," she said with a Gascon accent. Without the hat, I recognized her immediately. It was the pretty woman from Bordeaux whom Denise had pointed out to me in corrections, the one a man had married in order to pimp her out.

I looked at her without untying my own hat. The strange power of memories! She seemed like an old acquaintance, but she'd never actually seen me before. I wanted to ask her a host of questions, but we weren't alone. I tried on the hat she'd asked me to try and then asked her, if it weren't too much trouble, if she'd come see me in the shop across the street. She promised she would, and she kept her word. The next day she came to order a hat from me.

In true Bordelais fashion, she told me all her business. She was called la Belle Patisserie in Paris. I had heard of her. A gentleman had taken her in. Her husband, who no longer got his share of the proceeds, had her arrested. She'd denounced him to the police and separated from him to come live across the street at Madame Fond's, who rented out and furnished the house. She seemed like an excellent young woman, though she wasn't all that smart, and she was extremely blunt. I wanted to tell her that she'd gone from bad to worse with this woman. Maybe she already knew. I kept it to myself.

From that day on, she no longer passed by my shop without coming in. She had the prettiest face. She had settled in across the street, and two or three times she invited me to her table. This made me smile a little, and so as not to be difficult, one evening I finally accepted. I did not regret it.

After dinner at this house, they gamble, and the regulars arrive. These are incomprehensible beings. You rarely know their real names; they're baptized by the mistress of the house. One is called Major—who knows why—another the Commandant. All do their best to fight for hundred-sous coins. The women borrow the tiniest sums, up to fifty cents.

The old mistress of the house calls everyone *my dear*. She takes a cut from all the games, so whatever happens, she always does good business. The women of the house, however, generally have nothing. Those who would be very rich are broke. La Fond was buying the love she could no longer inspire on her own. She had her hair dyed, and she had false teeth. These required a lot of upkeep.

If a newcomer falls in with these people, the mistress of the house makes a thousand friends for him. She first gets him to play a little game. The stranger is surprised at all the politeness and reserve. For three francs, he's given a dinner easily worth ten francs. He admires this miracle of decorum and generosity. He's brought champagne, and they toast him, and the good times fizz and pop. Then the poor newcomer loses all he has on him—sometimes more—and he recognizes too late that he's been had.

Around the main feminine personage, other women flutter, some of them young and pretty. They serve the mistress, maybe by bringing people in, maybe by baiting the players. Those poor stooges win the smallest profits and they're thrilled. When they no longer have any money to bet, they bet the key to their room.

I remarked to my new acquaintance, who called herself Marie, that she was in a very sorry and dangerous society.

"I'm well aware," she said, "but what can I do? My husband is far away, but he could come back at any time. I don't know where else to go."

She wasn't wrong. A few days later, her husband did come to find her and force himself on her. He violently beat her. She came over to tell me her troubles.

"Don't you have any friends or parents whose house you could go to?"

"Non," she said to me as she cried, "I'm worthless. I've lived the life of a courtesan for six years. The poorest women are happier than me. What a miserable life! If I could go back to my parents' house, I would leave this instant."

I asked if she had written them.

"Non, I don't dare."

I begged her to do so, to make a clean cut.

This young woman had her day of reckoning. She had been both the object of women's envy and of men's passions. They saw her every evening in the window of a boutique, or in the corner of the Opera-Comique. Passersby would think she was lucky: she was covered in jewels, lace, and silk. That's what turns so many poor heads to becoming courtesans. No one could convince them of the reality of this life: shame and misery. It should be emblazoned on everything we're given so no one can be mistaken.

One morning, this Marie came to tell me that she had found a way to make a little money to return to her home, where her brother was waiting for her. She was going to throw a ball via subscription, at Provence, for twenty francs per ticket. She asked me to be in charge of it and all but made me promise to go. I told Deligny, who spread the word among his friends, including Médème.

One day, a servant with braided trim along every seam of his costume looked in at my door then entered. "Is this where Mlle Céleste lives?"

"Oui, monsieur."

He went back out and signaled to a carriage, which drove up in front of our building. It was a nice coupe with two horses. He opened its door, and an elegant lady descended gracefully, leaning on his arm. She had a veil so opaque that I couldn't see her face. She signaled to the footman to wait outside as she came into the shop, lifted her veil with one hand, and took my hand with the other.

"Lise!" I said, stepping back. She was so pale.

"What, no hug? You think I've changed?"

"Oui," I said, a little taken aback. "I'm shocked stiff to see you. You're so beautiful, and I didn't expect you—"

"If that's the reason, so much the better! Everyone thinks I'm ill, so I figured I must look different somehow."

I had her sit next to me. She was obviously in pain as she tried to hold herself up.

"Tell me everything," I said. "Where are you coming from?"

"Nice. I'd caught a cold. Ernest is so kind that he took it seriously. He loves me so much."

"Ernest—you're still with that wrinkly old count I dined with that one time on rue Saint-Georges?"

"Oui. I know you don't like him, but listen to what he's done for me. During his doctor's visits, he put it into Ernest's head that I was ill. He was wrong. But Ernest wouldn't let me go out after that, and I was bored. I didn't want to offend him, but I was depressed. That's what he took for illness." She coughed and went on, "He hired a traveling coach and sent me along, making me pass as his wife. Never has anyone been so kind, so thoughtful to me. It's a love like you've never seen. I'm not worried about the future. As long as Ernest lives, I'll lack nothing. He forbade me from seeing you, but he's traveling for several days. I can disobey him for you." She was pale when she came in, but as she talked, she flushed, and her eyes became bright.

I was afraid I was wrong, but something about her had changed that I didn't understand.

"I know what you're looking at," she said, laughing. "I've had all my top teeth pulled. See how pretty it makes me."

I grimaced, thinking of how much that must have hurt.

"I've adopted a little girl from Found Children during my travels. This will be my social circle."

"What?" I said. "But you don't have your own money. I thought you had to prove a certain level of income to adopt."

"It's not me they gave her to, it's Ernest, who is going to bestow an inheritance on her as soon as he returns and sees her in the nursery." This was certainly a unique fantasy, but she was so spontaneous that nothing she did surprised me.

La Belle Patisserie came in just then to advise me on the tickets for the ball. Lise took two for herself, jiggling a handful of gold coins in a pretty little purse. She had diamonds in her ears and on her fingers. *All right,* I said to myself, *she's truly happy. I'm glad for her.*

I asked her what she was going to do with the tickets, because I didn't think she would go to the ball.

"What am I going to do with them? Go with you and Eulalie, if that's all right."

"Eulalie is still living with you?"

"Oui, I bring her everywhere."

"And Camille?"

"He's always the same."

I saw her to the door. "I'll come around for you on Saturday," she said. And she got back into her carriage.

❧

When Saturday came, I was informed that a lady waited for me downstairs and that she couldn't come up the stairs.

When Lise, Médème, Deligny, and I arrived at Frères-Provençaux, everyone said "Oh!" at once.

I looked at Lise in the light. She was flushed. She gripped my hand to keep from falling. I sat her down.

"See, it's been a long time since they've seen me. They're astonished."

Frightened is what they were. Everyone walked by her and whispered. She had a pink mask decorated in the English style, and a black updo with roses.

She asked me several times, "Can you hear what

they're saying?"

"Non," I said. "They must be saying how well-dressed you are."

"Or that I look frightful." Turning to look at herself in the mirror behind her, she gasped.

"This is so hard for you," I said. "Why did you come?"

"Come on," she said, "be honest. Tell me that I'm no longer even a shadow of myself, that this fatigue, this numbness, is death."

"Are you crazy, my poor Lise? You can be sick without dying. Life hangs on tight."

"You think? It's just that I'm afraid of death."

Her eyes shone when she saw the dancers whirling about. She followed them with her soul. She seemed to inhale the life of others. They played a waltz, and she dragged herself upright. "I want to waltz."

I didn't dare contradict her and asked Médème to invite her to dance. I advised him to hold her up because I could see perfectly well that she would not last two turns around the floor.

"Oh, I can't," she said after a few moments with Médème, and she leaned against the wall. She coughed drily, and drops of blood came out of her mouth.

"How could you let her come?" Deligny said to me. "It's over for her."

"I didn't know she was so badly off. Besides, if I didn't come with her, she would have come alone."

"She'll make anyone who stays near her sick," said Médème. He lifted her in his arms and went down the stairs.

No one cared except Lagie, who said as they passed, "There goes Pomaré, who created this entire scene."

I took her home. She had a fever. She didn't want

anyone to undress her; she wanted to go back to the ball, to dance. Every light in her place was burning. I stayed part of the night. She remained done up, telling me random things, until fatigue overcame her and she fell asleep.

I went home very sad.

❧

The next day, I went to see her. She was up and even more ashen than the day before.

"Oh good, you're here," she said, her lips drawn. "You should be the first person I tell. Those bastards! I'll get revenge. They think I'm dead? Treason!"

I thought she'd lost her mind.

"This doesn't outrage you?" she asked me angrily.

"You haven't told me what happened."

"Fine. It turns out Eulalie is now Camille's mistress. They've both been fucking with me. He'll be of age in a few days, and she's running off with him. My heart did me wrong! I loved them both, and they're leaving me together. She told him so many terrible things about me, but I know his uncle, his tutor. I wrote to him, and I'll go see him in person if necessary. I can't let this affection for Camille go; it's the only pure thing I've had in my life. What nonsense it is to believe in eternal afterlife. The eternity is being alive. I'm not going to last much longer. He could have waited a little." She melted into tears.

I did my best to calm her down. "Hey, am I not your friend? I won't leave you. Your lover, this count, Ernest—I don't like him, I've made that clear. But in any case, didn't he give you ample evidence of his affection? Not everyone is as ungrateful as those two. Fuck them."

"Fuck them! I'd like to forget them. You're right."

She went on, "I saw my mother again. She came to see me in my hideout. I gave her things for my brothers and sisters. Eulalie was her favorite of course. She defends her, so I can't even talk about it with my own mother. I want Ernest to come back. I'm waiting for the doctor to come today. I won't tell him that I went out last night. My head feels like it's on fire! I'm going to bed."

We went into her bedroom. The room was all in yellow, as it had been on rue Saint-Georges, but this one was better furnished. There were two windows at the front hung with white and yellow curtains. Between the windows, a wooden pedestal held a plaster Virgin with a lace veil over it. You could see pearls and flowers strung across it. The fireplace faced her bed, whose head was turned toward the windows. There was a door at the bed's foot that opened onto an antechamber, and another door led into the salon.

As we entered by the latter door, the other door opened. "The doctor," announced her maid.

"I'll leave you," I said. "If I don't come tomorrow, then the next day, for sure." She squeezed my hand, and I exited.

When I returned, Lise's mother was there. She refused to let me in, so I came back a few hours later. She tried to forbid me again, but I insisted and entered.

Lise reproached me for going so long without seeing her. Her mother looked at me. I didn't dare say I'd been sent away. Her mother looked like Eulalie, and she disliked me.

Lise could no longer get out of bed. "I wish Ernest would come back," she said to me sadly.

I have to say it: this Ernest she was always waiting

on, I had run into him in Paris the day before.

"This is harder on me than this illness! I had already arranged so many things. They say that everyone is afraid I am dying. Everyone sent me notes."

"It's not that," I said. "It's that money is scarce. Everyone needs some."

"Maybe you're right. Ernest couldn't be late."

I took care of her. Her mother made me come in through the back entrance, saying, "You know her habits, her friends. You must know this monsieur Ernest is in Paris? He's been sent for many times, but he doesn't respond. The doctor he sent no longer comes. I don't dare tell her all this; she's still waiting. Last winter, they came to repossess things from the warehouse of the *Mère de famille*. I begged them to wait. He came up with three hundred francs for a pink mask. They came back after a few days. I don't know what to do."

"You have to stay out of it. I'll go."

She was charmed by this and let me see Lise when I wanted.

I told this proprietor of this warehouse that I would take care of the debt: if the worst happened and Lise died, her household was worth more than enough to pay everyone. They would want to wait until then to liquidate the warehouse's contents. The lady promised me they would.

I went back to Lise's a few days later.

"There you are! I'm doing much better! I hope to go out in a few days. I'm looking good, oui?"

I said yes without looking at her. She was sicker than ever.

Her mother came in and said to me, "Scold her. She likes you. She was up writing all night."

"Oui," said Lise with a strange smile. "Oui, that's what I did. I'm doing better, right?" Her eyes, which glimmered with fever, stared at me. I was forced to look at her. Her cheeks were sunken, her lips red. I heard her rattling breath. I wanted to weep.

Her gaze never left mine. I understood that she had something to tell me, but we weren't alone. Her mother never left us as long as I was there.

Lise took a little enameled watch from the night table and turned it between her fingers for a while. Then she gave it to her mother and said, "Here, take this downstairs to the proprietor. It's the last of my jewelry. What is taking Ernest so long to return? Not a letter from him! If I weren't waiting for him, I could be out spending time with friends. I'm sure he'll come see me, so I'd rather wait. Go quickly, Maman."

Her mother left. Lise pulled me near her bed and said, "I wrote to Camille's uncle. He wanted Camille to marry his daughter, so he will put a stop to this marriage with Eulalie. I am avenged! I just have to live long enough to see their response. You will tell Eulalie—if you are the one to tell her the story—that it was me." Someone walked toward the door. Lise put a finger to her mouth. Her mother reentered.

I told Lise how sorry I was to not have money to offer, to spare her these trips to Mont-de-Piété. I consoled myself by thinking that it wouldn't be for long. I lied to assuage her worries.

I left the room with a broken heart.

Several days later, they came to repossess items from her salon, her dining room, her bathroom. I was there. I made sure no one entered her bedroom. What they seized was enough to mostly cover the five hundred francs they were owed.

Lise asked who was walking around in the next room. I told her that some people wanted to see her rooms. She was always saying how she wanted to move, so this didn't surprise her.

"I'm going to leave this apartment. I'm going to move to the country." Then her eyes filled with tears and she repeated, "Oui, to the country. At Montmartre cemetery."

I did my best to chase this idea from her mind. It wasn't too difficult to do, because she was barely holding on to life. It make me feel worse when she kept her hopes up than when she spoke of her impending demise. I advised her to write to friends. No one came to visit.

M. Ernest, being informed that there were no more funds, had stopped bothering with her. Visits were useless, he said. He wrote that what she'd sold should last until the end. He didn't want to commit additional resources for someone who didn't have a month to live.

I told myself each day when I left the bedside of this poor girl, *Let her die before she's taken from her bed by force.*

She asked me for good wine, grapes, asparagus—all of which were out of season. Though I had little money, I procured what she desired. One day I arrived with my arms full. Eulalie opened the door, and I dropped everything on the floor.

She told me to go into the dining room, saying, "Don't go into her room; she's sleeping. I hope the devil tortures her, now that she's given herself over to him."

I didn't understand.

She went on, "You know what she did. Yesterday Camille's uncle came to see him, seemingly for a business meeting, and dragged him into his carriage almost by force. Lise caused all this. I received a letter this morning at the hotel: Camille bid me farewell. He informed me that he would send me money, and he repeated that he wanted to marry me. But here I am without any money, because I know him. Whoever speaks to him most recently is right, and Lise knew that perfectly well. I'll never see him again. In two weeks, he'll no longer think of me. He didn't take even that much time to forget his love for Lise. When she wakes up, I'm going to let her have it."

I begged her not to do that, to spare the last moments with her sister.

"What would that get me? I want her to die a month sooner."

Her mother, who had a weakness for Eulalie, appeared to be on her side.

That's when Lise rang. During this conversation, I had wished in my heart that she would stay asleep forever.

Eulalie opened the door at the foot of Lise's bed, and I followed. She leaned on the mantel, crossed her arms, and said, "It's me! Surprised?"

Lise took pains to raise herself onto her elbows, smile, and fall back again. "Finally!"

Eulalie approached her. "You're happy with your work, she-devil. Instead of repenting, you're wicked up to your last moment. Look at yourself. You're half dead. You won't get to bask in your triumph for long. I've been abandoned, but so have you. Your Ernest, he's in town. He no longer wants to see you, you who think you're beloved by all! Where are all your lovers now?"

Lise closed her eyes without answering. I saw tears pierce her eyelashes. Her mother pulled Eulalie back and signaled for her to be quiet. But she was definitely going to continue.

"Take her away," I yelled, "if you're the mother of both of them! And you, Eulalie, don't say another word. Have you no shame? Get out!" I didn't know what she might say, but I pushed her maybe a little too hard into the next room. I closed the glass-paned door behind her.

Lise grabbed my hand and said, "Stay with me. She's right, I've been abandoned by everyone—except for you. Why doesn't my lover come back?" She showed me her emaciated hands and arms. "The life that I led, it's a business. They bought a kiss, a night, from me; I had nothing more to sell, and they didn't want any more. You were smart to leave this life! After a while, everyone will forget your past. Maybe you'll forget it yourself and make friends. May the one who has been virtuous and honest be well paid at her final hour! Her best friend from girlhood cares for her up until the last breath, accompanies her to her grave, and weeps at her tomb. For women like us, there's nothing but mockery and insult during and after life. All the gold in the world isn't enough to make up for the last hours."

I wept.

"Why are you crying, my poor Céleste? Because I can see how things are today more clearly than I could yesterday? It's my sainted Virgin who inspired Eulalie. She made me understand that I lost so much time hoping for love I didn't deserve. Give me the rosary that's at the feet of the Virgin. Lift the veil that covers her and put her near me on this table. Look how her arms are open to all who come to her. Don't cry. Leave me, but don't go more than a day without coming to see me. Fetch a priest for me, or have my mother do it."

She leaned her had on the corner of the night table. The lamplight reflected off the alabaster Virgin and lit up Lise's face. She was quiet, and her eyes were closed. I thought it was over.

I closed the door gently. Her sister wanted to talk; I signed for her to be quiet. I asked her mother to find a confessor if she wanted him to arrive in time.

"How is she?" my mother asked when I got home.

"She's doing well," I said. "I wish it was me in her place." I went up to my bedroom as sad as I'd ever been.

※

The next day I went back to Lise's. I'd dreamed about her all night. I saw her dressed for a ball, wearing black flowers.

As I went in, I asked her porter how it looked. He gestured with his hand as if to say, *It's not all over, but it won't be long.*

I held my breath up three flights of stairs. I was about to ring when I heard laughing, talking. I knocked, and her sister came to let me in with a towel in her hand. I went into the dining room, where I saw oysters and wine. They were gaily having lunch in the room next to the dead.

I was furious.

"She's doing better, then?" I said, looking at the feast.

"Oui," answered her mother. "She's resting. Let her be."

"If she rests with all this noise that you're always

making, she must be sleeping her final sleep. Did she confess?"

"Oui, she saw her priest yesterday. It made her happy, and she asked forgiveness from her sister."

"It's about time," said Eulalie. "I told her she can keep her mercy. I'll never forgive what she did to me."

I went into Lise's bedroom. Her eyes were open, but she didn't move. I didn't dare get any closer.

Then she moved. I wanted to take her by the hand. She turned her large, dull eyes toward me and made a sign that she recognized me. Then she sighed without saying a word.

I sat in a chair beside her and asked how she was feeling. She nodded that she was fine. She had wrapped her rosary around her arm; her book of prayers was next to her. She moved her lips as if she wanted to speak to me. She looked around and made an impatient gesture. Then, summoning all her willpower, she said, "Listen."

I leaned in because her voice was so weak.

"I commissioned my portrait from a broke artist. He's almost done. No one wants to pick it up. Go find out about it. You keep it—you!"

I promised her I would.

She had just enough time to tell me the name of the painter: Montji. Words failed her anew. She signaled to me by pointing to her Virgin and kissing the cross on her rosary that she wanted to be alone.

I went out. I could no longer hold back my tears. I listened at the door as she tried to pray aloud. God alone could understand her thoughts.

The next day, when I returned, all the doors in the apartment were open. The soul had departed. A candle guarded the body. All eyes around her were dry.

I got to my knees at the foot of her bed and said a long prayer. I kissed her forehead and closed her still-open eyes. Then I left the room with my heart and eyes full of tears.

I didn't go home. I went to Deligny's. Seeing my grief, he cleared his schedule to distract and console me.

The day after that, it poured rain. I took a little coupe and went to rue Amsterdam. As I reached Lise's door, I heard her coffin being closed. I backed down the stairs. It seemed as if the coffin nails were entering my flesh. Her body was brought to the door.

The street was deserted, and the weather was awful. No one passed by. There were two people at her burial: me and the coachman who drove me.

When they had thrown the last shovelful of dirt over her, they erected a cross with her initials. I stood there with my feet stuck in the clay. It was as if part of me was in the ground with Lise. It took an effort to extricate myself. I was overcome. I heard voices calling me. I was afraid, and I left at a run.

Deligny was at my place when I got there. He reproached me for doing such harm to myself. This was more than I could bear. I cried for her and for myself. Wasn't the same fate in store for me?

I was at the cemetery a week later, hoping to find a headstone and a circle of friends. Nothing. Yet her mother had, by paying about 1,500 francs' worth of debt, taken over Lise's estate, which was worth about 15,000 francs. I had assumed that she wouldn't have had time to occupy herself with these affairs yet.

I came back to the cemetery after another ten days. Nothing.

They'd abandoned her now that she was dead as they'd abandoned her when she was sick. I commissioned an iron circle and a marble tomb inscribed with these two lines:

Here lies Lise, born 22 February 1825, died 8 December 1846. Her friend, Céleste.

I went to the artist Montji's. He gave me the portrait, reduced to two hundred francs instead of the usual price of three hundred. He was upset about her passing and made this sacrifice for me because I was Lise's friend. The portrait still hangs at my house.

These errands were out of my way, but I did them without resentment. Deligny helped me again in these circumstances. He was very good.

I recently went again to see Lise's tomb. I had sent notice, and it had been decorated with flowers. No one else had given it a thought for seven years. Some little newspaper had the courage to say nice things about this pathetic and lonely end: *Her life will be forgiven because she was so loved by so many.* They should have said, "Her life might be forgiven because she died a good Christian and she put up with so much from so many."

Lise had always endured a lot, really. Her death was a long and cruel agony. For several days at the end, her body had basically died while her mind lived on—and tormented her. I've never known anyone who had such a great fear of death. Under the influence of religious feeling—which she was faithful to all her life—she wanted to look her demise in the face to prepare herself for this terrible passage. That was her final wish, which itself scared her, because it made plain that all earthly hope was lost for her. She made a superhuman effort. She succeeded sometimes, but nature soon overcame her will, and she fell back into nervous spasms and heartbreaking fits of terror. Often during the night, she called for help. She had visions, and she cried out, "My God, let me live!" Then, I was told, her emaciated hand seemed to search for a friend in the emptiness. The poor girl who worked for her asked for her severance pay and quit to no longer be around these harrowing scenes.

I could never get used to the thought that I was the only one who cried for Lise. I bring up memories of our shared past life to find any heart that might sympathize with the grief that I carry for her. I think about Alphonse, who rekindled his life, his happiness, at her foolish fire. He took her death hard. That was maybe the only person she hadn't called—the only person who would have answered.

20.

A Supper at Café Anglais

THE DEATH OF LISE MARKS one of the saddest periods of my life. I fell into a deep depression. The ambitious hopes that had sustained me were erased. The excitement that would have carried me to the end of my days was sunk. My distaste for living hadn't diminished, only my ability to throw off the burden that is life was no longer the same. The misfortune I had suffered—this was absolute, undeniable horseshit. I thought so, at least.

I no longer believed in real affection. I only believed in the lover of the day, love without devotion and without a tomorrow. My soul was saturated by it.

I have often been reproached for having tormented those who loved me. If I did, I give myself this grace: I never acted out of spite or calculation. The doubt that ate at my heart was the only thing that drove my behavior, which could sometimes make me seem ungrateful or insensitive. Disbelief in the heart of a woman is a searing pain, but it gives her a strength and almost irresistible supremacy over others.

I then learned of news so strange that it left a real impression on me. It tied together ideas, feelings, and doubts that had been bouncing around inside me since Lise's death. The news was about the poor pianist I'd accused of being fickle while I'd derided myself for an instant of weakness and incredulity.

I learned that after we broke up, H… had fallen very ill, and medical science had been unable to determine the cause. He was advised to distract himself, so he left for Italy, visited Rome, became a Catholic, and entered a monastery. I had a hard time believing it, but I was assured it was true. His decision had been caused by the grief that he'd felt at our breakup. In any case, he had been inspired and said, while smiling at the person who told me this story, that if I damned all my friends that way, the Catholic Church owed me money. In the depths of my soul, however, I was more affected by this news than I wanted to let on.

I was horrified by my apartment. I hadn't ever been happy while living there, and I spent my nights elsewhere in order to not go back.

Deligny had gone back to his habit of squandering his money. I followed him down that path, and I talked loudly enough that I couldn't hear my sadness. My health had been profoundly changed by my attempted suicide. The fumes from a barrel of coal can't be swallowed without consequences. I coughed. I had a fire in my chest, so I drank champagne to extinguish it. I figured I'd die like

Lise did. But instead of making me afraid to approach death, I accepted it as a fact.

This frame of mind helped to even out my mood. I tyrannized Deligny. At any attempt at tenderness, I invariably responded, "You love me today, or at least you say so. When I fall ill, you'll leave me lying there like a dog. When I die, you won't give me a second thought." Nothing could dislodge this idea from my head.

I ended up succeeding in numbing myself. One dinner followed another; I no longer slept. I found rest in my memories.

In the middle of the messiness of this insane life, I linked up with a small woman who came into the shop. She was kind, spiritual, and spared not a thought for tomorrow. This woman was Brididi's mistress.

At first she detested me. She came to see me out of curiosity and then became attached to me. We became friends. She kept an eye on me to be sure that I wasn't spending my time with her dear Brididi, who had completely forgotten about me, I think. Deligny having left for M…, I found myself on my own and spent a lot of time with her. Her exuberance was inexhaustible, and her heart was good—maybe too good, because she had a great weakness for love. Brididi took advantage of this, a little. He was proud of inspiring such a great passion. He was right, mostly. She was truly charming: a lovely figure, pretty eyes, and curly hair that earned her the name Frisette.

What I liked best about her was her generosity. She helped anyone she could and hid the fact to avoid being repaid for it. If she only had six sous to take the omnibus, she gave them to a poor person and went on her way singing. If vivacity was lacking in my own head and heart, there were very excellent qualities to compensate. These qualities had shown up in me as vices. When in my madness I made any sense at all, Frisette listened and approved. I liked her very much.

I don't know which of us brought the other to a supper at café Anglais. I went, as I went to all these parties, because I had nothing better to do, even though it did not sound like much fun. If I had known that this party would have any direct influence on my life, maybe I would have prepared for its consequences.

At this supper, I found myself in familiar territory. I recognized many people that I had seen at Lagie's. The root of my character has always been seriousness. While others devoted their time to saying or listening to foolishness, I used that time to take account of the people nearby and to see what I could read based on how people looked.

My attention was fixed first on a young man of about thirty, tall, thin, brown-haired, pale. His forehead was ridiculously high, his face was long and narrow at the jaw. His eyes were large and black, his nose pointed, his mouth average, his teeth straight. He had taken off his coat, and I saw the sharp, narrow line of his shoulders through his shirt, which told me he was in bad health. He ordered the feast and spoke with the maître d'. Some women encircled him, and he spoke to them as if he was their protector.

While waiting to be served supper, he sat at the piano. He was a good musician, but he made too many faces and contorted himself theatrically while he played. His bony hands looked like spiders. I didn't compliment his playing, and he seemed surprised.

During the supper, he attacked me. He was clever,

but he had the sort of wit that can only be used against certain kinds of women. It was brutal and dishonest, and he didn't back away from a massive insult to get in a witty word. He always talked about himself and said he did everything better than everyone. His nobility was the best and his fortune the largest, and no one was as brave as him.

All these boasts worked my nerves. I didn't respond at all to his provocations, but I was primed to get angry. I'd already given him a nickname that I'd slid into the ear of my neighbor, who laughed heartily. He too applied it to the gentleman. I called him le Faucheaux, Daddy Long Legs.

What made my bad mood worse was that I'd been seated next to a large man—very handsome, and very pleased with himself—who did everything he could to draw my attention toward his large shoulders and barrel chest. He was stupid as a goose and vain as a peacock. This was a fop. Having my ear open to Faucheaux's sarcasm, I gave up on the pantomime of my neighbor, which put my neighbor in a worse mood.

This was already going badly. I still hadn't really said anything, and I already had two enemies.

Faucheaux seemed to be doing his best to get me to lose my patience.

I was very near to losing my manners.

The anger revealed my whole mind to me, and I started in with far more verve than I'd had in a long time.

"Monsieur," I said, "do you have the goodwill to leave me alone? I've been listening to your nonsense for an hour. By not responding to you, I thought you would comprehend that your wit was not to my taste. Spiders don't scare me, but they disgust me, and when they get too close, I crush them. So, great Faucheaux, do not bother me anymore, and I won't bother you."

This was harsh, but I had been cruelly provoked, and I have never radiated patience.

The epithet Faucheaux immediately set all those around me laughing. In all gatherings, small or large, there is a sense of justice that makes one's day. They got that by making me the object of his attacks, Faucheaux had allowed me the right—and the room—to respond rudely.

My adversary became furious. He didn't expect reprisals from one of these poor girls who were used to bowing their head under the yoke of opulent idiocy. He didn't take the time to consider that a chivalrous man never wins anything in a fight with a woman—especially this woman.

He bounced the ball back. "Who, then," he yelled, "brought along this—" and he debated so long on about what to call me that I didn't even care where he landed.

He maintained a haughty silence. Everyone could see that this was about to get fun.

This was the fashion, for the most part, at suppers arranged by Faucheaux. He found a victim toward whom he could spout his crude catechism. I had been chosen on this occasion, but with my personality, it was going to go down badly.

My handsome neighbor, who didn't have enough brains to avenge himself for these insults and punished me for my contempt of him, made common cause with my enemy and supported him with looks and gestures.

Only Frisette was unamused by this scene. The poor child understood that there was a massive thunderstorm coming to a head over my heart. She was afraid I would cross the line and thought that there was no way I could go ahead with this unsavory business. She came over to me and quietly begged me to get up from my seat and leave with her.

I sat her down and assured her at the top of my voice, "Why would I go? Monsieur is at his wit's end. Maybe I should not have come; that would be the first time that I've attended a supper with men of such good company. As monsieur said earlier, I came here freely, without any conditions. I'm not sorry, because I have been tactful and did not seek attention. Monsieur was not wise enough to imitate my reserve. He's probably not as used to high society as I am. Without a doubt, he is very noble—as of yesterday. He brings his conquests very low to lift himself up. If there weren't women like us, where would he live, at the Jardin des Plantes? I've paid for my echo in listening to him. I'm staying."

I definitely hit home. He was indeed an upstart. He turned ashen and pressed his lips together. I think he began to regret attacking me.

I had won an ally during the heat of the discussion who, touched by my bravery, joined my cause and broke off a lance in my favor. It was a young man who I've not yet mentioned, though he certainly merits my attention more than anyone else present.

Addressing himself to Faucheaux, who appeared to know him well, he said, "My dear friend, I don't recognize your usual good taste and generosity today."

"If I wounded mademoiselle's pride," answered Faucheaux, who thought he saw an honorable way to retreat, "I am ready to offer reparations. You know quite well, my dear friend, that if I make the mistake of teasing the girls, I have the *good taste* to pay them. Since you've declared yourself her knight, set the ransom."

"Fifteen louis."

"Fifteen louis! So be it. It will be there tomorrow."

"Tomorrow! That's too late," said my champion, who showed himself to be merciless. He knew that Faucheaux was freer with his words than his actions.

"I don't have it on me."

"Doesn't matter. Vesparoz will lend it to you."

There was no way to take it back. Faucheaux's pride was at stake. He rang, and Vesparoz, the maître d', appeared.

"Bring me fifteen louis," Faucheaux said.

The maître d' went out, and a boy came in carrying a platter with the requested sum.

"Pay this money to mademoiselle Céleste."

Naturally I refused to take it. But my champion wouldn't hear of it. He had decided to push the joke to its limit and punish Faucheaux for his bad taste.

"Bring it to me," he said to the boy. He put the fifteen louis on the table at the place beside him. Then he turned to me. "My dear child, come sit next to me."

I did as he wished.

"Take this," he said. "It's for you. You can't refuse without insulting your champion and dealing me a mortal blow. These are the rules of war." He turned to Faucheaux. "Now, go on as you please, included in this price. When you've said as much as your fifteen louis will buy, I will ask you to not ruin the rest of the evening."

Faucheaux seemed to think this good advice, because he got up and extended his hand to me. "Let's make peace."

There was no hesitation. I put my hand in his graciously enough.

At the end of this moment, the scene took a turn that I did not expect. I had new evidence that when it comes to emotions, the extremes touch. Often one is close to loving women that you believed you hated. When we left the table for music, dancing, and singing, Faucheaux pulled me into a corner of the room and confessed that he'd created that ridiculous scene to get my attention and then to have a reason to make it up to me.

I answered him politely but coldly, saying that if he set up women he liked that way, I didn't know what he would come up with for those he didn't like.

He became sweet, insistent. He promised me mountains and marvels.

I didn't have it in me to make nice at this point. I listened to him distractedly.

On the other hand, I was very attentive to my ally, whom, for reasons known only to me, I will call Robert, which is not his real name. He noticed that he was the subject of my attention, and he approached us.

With flirtatious femininity, I loudly repeated the words that Faucheaux had come over to say quietly. I wanted to seal my victory and said to Faucheaux, "I see that you've come to your senses, and I think you're sincere. Also, rest assured that I do not want you. I just met you yesterday, and I don't see any reason to prolong our relations." And I left him in the corner, ashamed of and agitated by the confession he'd made to me.

Faucheaux took a bottle of champagne and emptied it in one go. I should give him credit—I'd never seen anyone drink like that without throwing up. Was it bravado or to soothe himself? I'm convinced it was the latter.

Most of the time, boastful types are at bottom the tenderest and weakest people. They make noise to overwhelm others, and the eccentricities they use to amuse the public are only a show. Lift the curtain, and behind it you'll see them playing out the drama of their heart, which is often sad and gloomy.

But I don't have anything at all to give. I have my poverty.

Robert didn't leave my sight. I followed all his movements from where I stood. When he chatted with a woman, I wanted to insert myself between them.

I sat by Frisette and arranged myself in a way so that she would talk about him to me.

He was about twenty-eight, tall enough, fit and well-proportioned, with a domed head and lovely brown hair, a fine pale complexion, a medium forehead, an oval face, long eyelashes, and a full mustache. His brown eyes were ordinary in their size but their gaze was deep and penetrating. He had elegant manners, he was well-dressed without being stiff and self-conscious like so many young men. His wit was quick. His personality seemed a bit rash, but he knew to keep himself in check and reined in his spirit with charming manners.

I looked at him and saw all this. I always looked at him.

"Without him," I said to Frisette while pointing him out, "I don't know how this argument would have ended. He did me a great favor. I don't know if I thanked him."

I wanted him to come speak to me…but he didn't. My heart took as many turns around the room as he did without his noticing it.

They improvised a ball, but he didn't ask me to dance. However, he watched me.

The tall gentleman who'd been my neighbor at the table had persuaded himself that my coolness was a game. With the tact he was known for, he asked me loudly if I wanted to leave with him. I got up and walked away without answering.

Faucheaux didn't say anything more to me, but he picked up on what had passed between us, and he seemed sorry.

This promenade of my eyes and heart in the wake of M Robert made me tired. I went straight up to him and asked if he wanted to drive me home, to take me away from these two gentlemen.

"Oui," he said, turning a look on me that seemed to read my thoughts. "Oui, in ten minutes. First I want to dance with you."

A waltz began. He set me spinning without waiting for an answer. I was fluid; I could feel his nervousness in his arms, and he clutched at me. I felt the beating of his heart. I inhaled his breath. I closed my eyes and let him lead. I swooned with a happiness that passed through me like a lightning bolt but that I'll always remember.

I returned to Frisette radiant.

She knew Robert, or had come to learn more about him, because she told me, "That's the comte *** you were dancing with." This name was too grand, too far from where I was. I became despondent.

"Are you coming?" said Robert. "I'm going to take Frisette home first, then you."

"I'm sorry to have bothered you."

He gripped my arms and said, "It's my pleasure. I wouldn't have dared ask you. I didn't want to be the third man to accost you tonight."

He promised to come see me that afternoon at four o'clock. I went home, head and heart filled with his face. Foolish that I'd been despairing for my life!

At age twenty! Is that even possible? The day before, it had seemed to me that life was no longer my goal. How pathetic. Today I feel reborn in hope. I foresee new horizons, new worlds. My wings have unfurled.

21.

Robert

I was, by happy accident, free from all material worries for the moment. I could, for a little while anyway, live out my dreams and build myself castles in Spain.

Time seemed to stretch on for ages that afternoon—until four o'clock. To make it go faster, I went down to my shop across the street. Several days before, I had written to my friend in Holland. I found myself daydreaming about getting a letter from him. He sent me a note for two thousand francs to cash at a bank on rue d'Hautville. With these two thousand francs, plus my three hundred francs, I was very rich.

I went to the door of the shop to leave, but a snarl of carriages barred my way. A fancy phaeton pulled by two black horses was waiting to turn onto rue Geoffrey-

Marie. The impatient horses reared, and one of the servants jumped down.

"Hold on, hold on," said the young man who held the reins. He calmed the horses and unhooked his carriage with infinite skill.

When I saw that he was out of danger, I crossed the street to go up to my place, but fate prevented me from getting home. Robert was about to ask for me in the lobby when he saw me.

"Bonjour, my dear child. Did you sleep well?" Then, after he'd really looked at me, "You look like you've seen a ghost! Are you ill?"

"Non, but I was frightened when I saw you turning onto this street from fauborg Monmartre with all these carriages. Your horses are upset."

He laughed and offered me his arm to go up to my place. I was embarrassed when I was near him. I thought of myself as so far below him that I didn't dare look him in the face. My embarrassment was even more ridiculous since he was kind and chivalrous.

"I won't come with all my horses," he said, "since it scares you. I don't know this quarter well. I'm staying on rue de Grenelle Saint-German. I rarely come down rue Geoffrey-Marie. But if you'll allow it, I'll come here often."

I was reserved in my responses. Though she may be lost—or she was at one time—the woman in love locates within her own past a memory of modesty, of purity. I loved him.

I wanted to lift my gaze a little, but this was not possible. The scene at dinner the day before, the insults I'd said, came hurtling back into my memory—along with my name, Mogador, and my entire life as a courtesan and performer. I had nothing to give him. Nothing at all.

"I embarrass you, maybe?" he said and got up to leave.

"Non, non, stay." There was a prayer in these words.

He sat back down and began to chat. "Do you know, Céleste, that I've known you a long time? I often saw you at the Hippodrome, and every time I admired your skill and bravery."

I realized that he'd found something of merit in me: bravery! I had been brave, because I was horribly afraid of horses. When I rode, nervous tremors shook my limbs, and I commanded myself, like a general who's startled when he hears gunfire: "Shake, shake, you pathetic carcass! If you knew where I was going to take you later, you'd tremble even more." I didn't know then that all these efforts to ride a horse would be more than paid for by a word from him.

"Would you like to dine with me this evening?" he asked.

"Oui, if you don't have anything better to do."

"Be ready at six o'clock."

⁂

One day, a couple of weeks later, he came to get me with one of his carriages. It was a lovely double coupe in blue silk, so small that we both could barely fit. I hunkered down inside the carriage.

"Are you afraid of being seen?" he said.

"Oui, afraid for you."

We dined at Deffieux's. My heart was heavy; this love was like a vision that was going to take flight any second then drop back down into the darkness. The friendlier Robert was, the more I believed I'd watch as the vision vanished.

He took me home, and we spent the evening at my house. I loved him too much to lie to him. I told him all that I had done, all that I had been.

"Others have told you all this," I said, "my enemies. Maybe you regret giving me a kind word, a kiss. I love you, Robert. I've loved you for a long time. Being near you makes me lose my senses. I want to undo the past, but that's impossible. Do you want my present?"

His response was a wonderful kiss. It was as if another woman came awake inside me.

He didn't like the quarter where I lived; it was too far away. *If I were nearer,* I said to myself, *I would see him more often.* I decided to rent an apartment on place de Madeleine. I gave the shop to my mother. I was so impatient to be nearer to Robert that at the risk of making a huge dent in my savings, I paid double, ensuring that my lodgings would be ready for me to move into as soon as possible.

Robert gambled sometimes. He gave a party for some friends in an apartment that he had on rue Bleue. Lagie came to the party with me; the supper was magnificent. All through it, everyone spoke of a woman named Zizi, who was in the country. They laughed about it and looked at me. I didn't understand.

"Who is this Zizi?" I asked Lagie.

"That's his mistress, and this is her house. He sent her to the country."

My whole head turned crimson. When they came to clear the table, I went straight to Robert and asked him if what they'd told me was true, if I was at his mistress's house.

"Not exactly," he said. "It's true that a woman I've known for a long time, and who I cannot get away from fast enough, lives here. But you're at my house. I'm going to leave her, but I want to be sensitive in how I go about it. I'll leave everything that's here to her."

They'd begun to gamble, and they played a great game. I sat there a long time without seeing, without hearing, sunk inside a single thought: he had a mistress! For two weeks, he had only given me his spare time. I couldn't be anything more to him than a whim, a will o' the wisp, ashes he was going to throw into the wind. I had to break it off, but I didn't have the courage. I did my best to forget her at all costs. Robert lost a lot of money at the table; that was fine with me.

One of his friends who was sitting near me said, "Robert's nuts! I don't know how he can do it. He has a lot of debts, and his father is still young. He'll be broke before he inherits."

This made me happy. A secret premonition told me that his losing everything would punish him for me.

There were races at Versailles the next day, so no one went to bed. At six in the morning, a harnessed wagon with four horses was at the door, along with other carriages requested by the gentlemen.

One carriage remained empty.

"Do you want to come?" Robert asked me.

I wanted to refuse, but I didn't have the guts. I climbed in despite myself to keep an eye on him.

The races ended, and he came over to tell me goodbye. He was leaving for Saint-Germain, where he had business, but he promised to visit the next day. His friends, who knew enough to wonder what kind of business took him to Saint-Germain, wanted to do him a favor. They invited Lagie and me to dine in Saint-Germain. I was too far gone to decline.

❧

We arrived at the Henri IV pavilion. Robert, on seeing me, jumped up. Those who'd brought me began to laugh.

"Why did he run out of here?" I asked.

Georges, who laughed like a child, said, "He's between two flames. Zizi is here, but whatever. You'll dine with us. I'm going to say that you're my mistress."

The idea of playing this scene out disgusted me. I hid from this woman like a thief. I'd been begging for a look, waiting for a stolen kiss from a man who belonged to another. I was sorry I came.

Robert was informed that I'd accepted the invitation from his friends and that I knew everything. He came over and clasped my hand, which remained cool and dry in his.

We were seated at the table. I wasn't hungry, but I had a powerful thirst. My gaiety turned to cynicism. Robert looked at me, and I pulled my hand free. I angled my neck toward my neighbor, who kissed me.

Robert sat opposite me, fixing his gaze on mine and signing for to to me to leave the table. I obeyed, as always despite myself. But it was time. I was about to suffocate.

He took me to the far end of the garden, sat me down, and took my hands. "What's going on, Céleste? You seem to want to torment me for fun. Yesterday you loved me; at least, that's what you said. If you don't love me anymore, can't there still be a little interest? A little affection? If you have any love for me, don't spread it around to everyone else."

"What would you like me to do? Don't you have a mistress? Do you want me to weep in front of her? I'm free. I want to have fun and forget you." I dissolved into tears.

"Forget me? Why? Is it my fault that before I knew you, I already had a mistress? Did I force you to come here? And finally, as long as you are here, haven't I kept you apart from this woman? I didn't say a word to her. Stay. You'll see that my room here is far away from hers. I love you. I don't love her. I'm not going to be cruel and leave her without giving any reason. Please."

He kissed me, and all was forgotten.

All night long, I listened to hear if his door opened.

Zizi stayed in the country, and I went back to Paris without taking my eye off Robert.

I was afraid he'd be angry. I loved him too much. It was exhausting. He loved society and went often to balls or to parties with young people. I didn't want him to sacrifice these pleasures for me.

⁂

One day the comte de S… came to invite me to the ball given every year at Frères-Provencaux by the Jockey Club. He made me promise to go. I accepted so I would have an occasion to annoy Robert.

On that very same day, Robert told me that he had a party at a friend's house to go to. I thought he was lying. I offered to skip my ball if he would stay with me. He refused.

I waited for him to come back, hoping that he'd change his mind. He rang, and I opened the door.

But it was the comte de S… who had come to pick me up, along with his friends. He told me that they weren't leaving without me. I spent ten minutes getting ready and followed them out the door.

This was the first time I'd been invited to this ball. It was not the kind of place most women were welcome. Only actresses were invited, and kept women—all of whom will rip you to shreds with their beautiful teeth. It's the same with this class as with any other, only the price is different. When the headlining queens were seen arriving at the same time, they threw themselves at the gate face first. They said it was a fate worse than being hung from a scaffold to enter together. If anyone had said to them in advance, "We've invited Mogador," they would have leapt up, saying, "The horror! We aren't going!" But no one had told them. It was a bouquet saved for them by those tired of their laughable vanity.

When I entered, there was a general hurrah. The women retreated to the corners, and the men came up to me. They wanted to see me face to face. Without a lovely girl called Brochet, who remembered that before arriving under these golden-paneled halls she had been a laundress, I would have danced with two men at a time. The other women were scandalized. They were clustered and whispering.

I heard, "Mogador! A rider from the Hippodrome! A woman who danced at the public balls!" They knew this was my way to make money and found me unworthy of their company.

This contempt would have put me in a fury if I hadn't been convinced they were jealous—and for good reason. I had my consolations: the most distinguished men, the most well-born young men, were charming toward me, which compensated for the scorn of the women.

Among them, meanwhile, there was one who proved herself to be less of a snob. They called her Chouchou, and I liked her very much. She was indefatigably witty. I was seated near her, and she was very friendly toward me.

"It annoys the hell out of me," she said, "to see all these snobs turn up their noses. Here, look at these two sisters. Last year they were only too happy to share supper and the little iron bed of a poor boy who'd picked them up at the docks. They got work in a theater, where they were given a letter proving how young they were. To maintain this illusion, one must have a very short memory. Over there is Verveine. She simpers behind her fan to hide her bad teeth. For four years, she was a servant from the Panoramas. I still remember her in her clogs, cleaning the shop one morning. She undoubtedly has convinced herself that she is the daughter of a grand family."

Chouchou had energy. She went on for a long time and gave me a biography for each of these women. I thanked her, because it was likely that I was destined to make the rounds of this scene, and it's good to know who is whose mistress. I had hoped to make Robert jealous by going to this ball, but I lost the need. He asked me if I had fun. I told him yes.

Deligny was back from his tour of the countryside, and he learned of my new liaison. Since he understood, he no longer came around, but he was hurt by it.

One day, when I went to Enghien with Robert, we heard a loud noise in a room on the first floor. Geniol, who knew me, came to beg me to leave. He told me that Deligny was upstairs with a bunch of his friends, and that he seemed to have noticed me in the garden with

Robert. He drank to me in jest, but then he had a fit and smashed everything.

"Go," Geniol said to me. "He's a good boy, and he's always loved you. Avoid making a scene."

I wanted to go see him, but Robert held me back, so we left. I had a broken heart and was miserable all evening.

The next day, I sent for news. The response came that Deligny was ill. He'd apparently made a great effort to forget about me, but with no success. He had enlisted and left for Africa. I'm often blamed for his departure; they say I was the cause of his downfall. This accusation is very unfair. I never asked anything of him. If he'd followed my advice, he would have been more frugal. Besides, leaving for Africa turned out to be lucky for him—he found a glorious career. He judged me less severely than everyone else did out of pity for him. When he returned to France, his first thought was to come take my hand. He was a brave boy! More stubborn than loving.

As soon as he had returned from M…, he had rushed to my house. I bluntly told him all about my liaison with Robert. He didn't blame me. He only blamed himself.

"It's my fault," he said. "I didn't know how to make you love me." His blue eyes were full of tears. He said as he left, "I got exactly what I deserve. Poor girls loved me, and I treated them terribly. They told me, 'Your day will come.' They were right; you avenged them. Goodbye, Céleste. Try to be happy. I'll never love another woman. Later, much later, maybe you'll come back to me. When that happens, my heart will be open. Goodbye." And then he'd fled my rooms.

I didn't see him again until the day at Enghien when Geniol told me, "Leave, he cannot stand your presence."

I often spoke of Deligny. Robert wanted to pull me away from this memory, as it made him jealous. I noticed this about him, so I came back to this memory constantly. That's how the heart is made. It's nice to have a victim to sacrifice to your idol. It's a widespread savagery that exists everywhere, among all classes. If we don't have the ability to give ourselves to those we love, we give them a trophy made of the hearts we broke. The heart of our lover attaches to another and grows larger. To be young and pretty isn't enough to succeed in love.

The harvest takes a long time. Some are more skillful at it than others. They say that courtesans don't have a heart—that's silly and insulting. It's in the human condition to have one from the same material, stone, or bronze, or marble! Meaningless words! The heart doesn't wear away; it changes how it feels but always fights until God stops the ticking of life's clock. Everyone has one heart, and only one. Those who buy a kiss and give their gold along with their heart, do they think they're buying souls? They only pervert the whole enterprise. A woman can sell ten kisses; she can't give ten hearts. Stop spoiling women through luxury and vanity and jealousy, and you'll see that they're all capable of honest feelings. The women who've fallen the farthest feel a flutter in their heart when they're in love. That love has been asleep beneath disgust, but no matter. It wakes up when it's called by destiny.

I wanted to make myself grand like the rest of this class so that Robert would love me. I hitched my life to his. I wanted to annihilate my past. Whenever I had to wait for him, I was worried. I imagined a thousand possibilities. I thought he was at another woman's house. Hours spent without him were hours of my life lost.

When I would see him at last, all was forgotten. He would tease me. It amused him to see the advance the sway that he held over me.

Though he still didn't have his full inheritance, he spent enormous sums and ran up debts like many young men from families of means. I was a drop in his foolish bucket. On the first day I'd seen him, he'd given me a ring.

I loved the good in him. We sometimes went out together in the evening. I was proud, happy to the point of forgetting the past and the future both. I clamped myself against him. I loved him too much for him to love me or even notice. You know someone loves you when your mistress always waits for you, she follows you with her eyes, and a word from your mouth brings her joy or pain. You create it, and you abuse it. Several months passed like this. Every day I loved him more so that he wouldn't feel indifferent toward me.

<hr />

My attempted asphyxiation had left me with very inflamed bronchial tubes. It hurt to breathe.

"Take care of yourself!" Robert said to me.

"Oh, please," I responded. "I'll live a long time on your love."

One morning, his valet came looking for Robert at my place. "Monsieur the count must come quickly," he told me. "Monsieur the marquis is very ill."

Robert blanched when he heard. "My God! My father!"

He followed his servant out without telling me goodbye. My heart clenched. I felt something bad was on its way.

Several days passed without news. It felt like a century. I had run out of courage and patience. That evening I went to the door of Robert's building. I looked, knew he was there, and went home very calmly. I wrote to him about how worried I was.

Finally I received a letter in return. I looked at it from all sides without daring to open it. It was from him, but what did it say? It took a huge effort to take it out of the envelope.

> *My dear child, thank you for thinking of me. I'm feeling terrible. When can I see you? I don't have any idea. A frightening illness has taken me out. While I've been expecting it for a long while, I didn't think it was so close.*
>
> *You understand that this is an illness that requires isolation.*
>
> *Robert*

That was where the letter ended. My tears had dried so I could read better. He didn't love me. This was goodbye. Life left me.

That's impossible, I told myself. *In a few days, he'll come back. I'll see him again. Nothing is ever over between us.*

I waited a few days, I breathed in all the noise from outside. I heard passersby, carriages. I wanted to go out to distract myself, but if he came during my absence…. So I stayed home.

I no longer believed in anything. Living on hope every day was antithetical to my very nature.

One day I went to my mother's house, but she had closed the shop and gone out with Vincent.

So I went to Frisette's. She consoled me, telling me

that in a moment like this, with mourning so recently in his heart, Robert couldn't have taken up with another mistress. He had obligations to fulfill. According to her, I was foolish to torment myself this way. Frisette seemed so much wiser than me, and she was right. I took confidence and went home feeling a little calmer.

Two of Robert's friends came to see me some days later.

"Well," one of them said to me, "Robert's going to inherit. That's good news for you."

"Good news for her? That's not a sure thing," said the other, who was called Georges. "He's going to leave town to mourn at the country estate, and then he'll have to think about marriage."

"Have you seen Robert?" I asked.

"Yes, at church," said the first. "He looked awful. He was pale, and his eyes were red. He loved his father very much, but his death was the luckiest thing to happen to him."

"Is it ever lucky to lose your father?" Georges asked, looking at him.

"Sure—when you have debts. His father was worth four thousand livres a year, but he had four or five children. Robert will still have a decent inheritance. He won't let this go, Céleste."

I was broken by all that I'd heard. At first I only understood one thing: that Robert was going to leave Paris. But that last sentence snapped me out of it. I straightened up to tell them that I didn't love him for his wealth.

They laughed at me and took their leave, saying, "All

the same, he won't let his inheritance go, Céleste."

I stood there stunned. To take even a step toward Robert was not possible without making him think I had an ulterior motive.

My distress began to join my new embarrassment. I had moved because of him. I was living in my new apartment. To make the move possible, I had spent quite a bit of money. He didn't know, and I wouldn't have told him for anything in the world.

Robert left the city without saying goodbye. I was desolate. I didn't even know his address; I only knew that he was removing himself to some place where he wanted to keep his share of the land.

I went back to Frisette's and told her, "I want to forget him. It's thankless. Come on, let's go to parties and have fun."

We spent the night gambling. My health deteriorated, and I wasn't able to forget him.

Georges came back. He found me so depressed, so changed, that he took pity on me. He said, "If you love him so much, write to him. Here's his address."

When I was alone, I read and reread this address a hundred times. I couldn't see clearly into my heart, and I didn't know at all if I wanted to write to him or not. I started ten letters, and I ripped them all up. *Non*, I said to myself, *not until I have money, a lot of money*. If he came back, if he saw the poverty I was living in, he would think I was needy. He'd throw me a few louis and leave again.

I often gambled at the bordellos, at the gaming tables. I would go to hell to catch some luck, because I would have liked to make a fortune. But the game treated me badly. I made the acquaintance of a Russian prince—young, handsome, rich, sweet! He liked me, but

I couldn't hide my indifference toward him.

When I'd paid the most pressing debts and saw some money in front of me, I wrote to Robert. I was happy for all of two hours. I would suffer for four months.

In writing to you, my friend, I don't want to blame you for being interested in me. I loved you. It's not much of a thing, a love like mine. You have the right to walk all over me. You've stomped on my heart, and it bled a long time. Since you left, I've been throwing myself into gambling dens. I was only able to kill your memory after I'd exhausted myself.

Today, when this letter reaches you, I am asking your forgiveness. You never said goodbye to me—not a word. It would have been humane. I never want to make you out to be evil. If you had listened in your solitude, you would have heard my soul crying out to you.

I'm crazy to love you like this. I know very well that you can't be with me. With a sane word, I would cure myself of this feeling. You've broken me without even thinking about it. Never do this, Robert. It's horrible. I'm sick. I've moved beyond sorrow—or, rather, my sorrows pile up.

Life is a book that turns a page every day. I wanted to stop at the chapter about our love because it lifted me up a little in my own esteem. I didn't know I was capable of such love.

I don't want to lure you here or tell you that I'm waiting for you. In order for me to write this to you, it all has to be finished between us.

I don't need anything. I'm almost rich. I wish you all the happiness in the world by forgiving your forgetting.
Céleste.

I put this letter in an envelope and dropped it in the post. I counted the hours of its journey. At the moment when he should have received it the next day, I put my hand to my heart to stop its beating.

Lucky letter! He was holding it, maybe reading it. I hid my weakness from everyone. To Marie alone, my maid, to this girl who had saved my life, I spoke of him. A flower, a faded bouquet, became a treasure.

I hadn't requested a response, but I waited for one.

⁂

Marie came into my bedroom the next day. There couldn't be a response yet, but I looked at her hands anyway. She had nothing, she just seemed embarrassed. I asked what she wanted.

"Sorry, madame, but I don't know how to tell you this."

"What?" I said impatiently.

"Madame is such a good person. Here it is: I have a sister who is seventeen. She came to Paris to learn a trade, but she ran away. I don't know what she did, but she was arrested. My mother granted me the power to reclaim her at the prison where she's locked up. She gets out tomorrow; I don't know what to do. She wants to enter a brothel, but my mother doesn't want her to."

"Your mother doesn't want her to? She's smart."

"I want to ask madame's permission to let her stay in my room, upstairs, until I can find a job for her or my mother comes to find her. She's going to return in service to Choisy-le-Roi."

"My poor Marie, I would be glad to, but she can never come down to the apartment. My life is not steady enough that I can openly receive a woman under false pretenses."

Augustine—that was the name of her sister—got out the next day and came to my place. Marie had her come into my bedroom. She was a tall girl, thin, with a delicate face and almost blond hair. I thought that this poor girl, shut up alone on the fifth floor in a little room, was going to die of boredom.

I told Marie to keep her in the attic kitchen all day, which was big and as long as the entire apartment. She could mend the linens, and I would give her a wage each day, and she would be fed until she was placed. She seemed thrilled.

Once day, we received a letter from their mother announcing her impending arrival. I was fine with seeing Augustine go. I had watched her face; she wasn't completely honest. Her face was brazen, and she was lazy. I had bought two dresses of India cloth, and it took all the convincing in the world to get her to sew her own.

Meanwhile she paid me her debt of gratitude without even knowing it. It was Augustine who, while running an errand, brought me a letter from Robert that the concierge had mislaid. I hugged her out of sheer joy. I shut myself in my room, sure that no one could see me. I kissed the writing, the envelope.

My dear Céleste, I didn't answer you sooner, though I very much wanted to. You don't have to see me; believe me when I say that I have a thousand things to remember you by and that you'll always have a place in my affections. But my dear child, you know my position now. I have interests too serious to be neglected. I'm obligated to sacrifice my present games for my future position. I'm glad to know that you're well off. I knew that I was condemned to forgo happiness, but I will certainly never be as happy as when I was near you. I know that you're suffering; I get news from Paris.

If, as you told me, you have some affection for me, you'll take care of your health. It's most precious to me. When you love, you try to make someone else happy. Show yourself that kind of care.

I'm waiting for one of my friends. My old castle is going to scare him; it's quite somber. The countryside and its views are superb, but I think that these are too small to make a case for the place. But I love this sadness and this solitude. I feel a melancholic joy being away from the rest of the world. The coldest imagination becomes poetic in this gorgeous setting. I live in one of the old towers of the chateau. My window overlooks the magnificent wildflowers in the meadows, with the Indre running through the middle. The horizon is enclosed by woods and splendid forests. If I were a painter, I would send you sketches of my chateau. We love to guess what's inside the people we're thinking about, almost follow them from afar.

Finally, my dear child, my life is now all for the sake of others, and I am trying to forget a too lively past.

Goodbye, my poor friend. Forgive me my rudeness. I had to write you one last time just for the pleasure of it. Take good care of yourself. Keep a place for me in your memory.

Sending you kisses.
Robert.

This letter burned my fingers and my eyes. I looked for a word of tenderness. I only found indifference and cold reason.

Come on, I said to myself through tears, *it's all over. All the effort I made was for nothing. Just reading his name, I feel that I love him more than ever! What am I going to do?*

Marie came in, telling me that her mother would arrive in two days. The poor girl was so attached to me that she wept when she saw me. She tried to console me. I had a little fever, so I stayed in bed.

Augustine left without saying anything to Marie, and she took Marie's nicest bonnet and her silk apron. Marie was worried. She had reason to be, because Augustine didn't come back. She ran off. Her mother arrived. This was, I think, the event that made Augustine flee. She had told her sister that she didn't want to go back with her mother. The poor woman, who hadn't seen Augustine in a long time, left disappointed for Choisy-le-Roi, where they were waiting for her.

Three days after Augustine took off, Marie brought me a letter that she had received but that she didn't understand. Over the address, it said, "To Mademoiselle Marie, care of Mademoiselle Céleste." The stationery read, "Hotel-Dieu Hospital."

Mademoiselle, if you could within the next twenty-four hours identify a person named Augustine...deceased yesterday at four o'clock in the afternoon.

I read it just fine, but I didn't comprehend it any more than Marie. It must be an error. I told Marie to go visit the ward that was mentioned. It wasn't possible her sister was dead.

The poor girl went insane. She begged me to come with her. I didn't dare refuse.

When our carriage arrived at Hotel-Dieu, I presented the letter, and we were taken into an office. It was indeed Marie they had requested to speak to. A young girl had been brought in two days before and died the next day. Also, said the orderly, you're going to have to identify her.

"Go ahead," I said to Marie. "I'll wait for you here."

"Madame!" she cried. "Don't leave me alone. Come with me."

"Come now, my girl, be brave. Don't cry like that. You'll make me upset. I'll go with you."

We crossed a windowed gallery and went down a few stairs. As they opened the mortuary, I heard a strange noise. The waves of the Seine were hitting the wall as they flowed by. Along with the wind, it sounded like whispering voices. The door was opened, and a cold damp touched our faces.

I was afraid. I took a step back, and poor Marie did too. The day was dim, so the guard lit a large candle above the stairway. My eyes became accustomed to the obscurity of the mortuary and I could see. It was long, lit by paned windows, like those in a cellar, along one side. Starting right in front of the entrance, on both sides, were stone beds as far as the eye could see. Some were flat, while others had domed covers.

"Come on," the guard said to us, putting his hand in front of the light to illuminate our way and protect it from the breeze.

I took Marie's hand. We were at the fourth slab. The man stopped, gave me the candle to hold, and lifted the cover. It was a willow lid covered with waxed fabric. I held the light higher.

"See if this is her," said the man.

"Madame," said Marie, grabbing my arm, "that's not my sister."

I held the candle over the cadaver of a woman whose illness had wasted her away. This was a skeleton covered with blueish skin. I would never have believed someone could reach such a state of emaciation. When Marie touched me, my heart jumped, and it kept me from saying a word. All the covered slabs were occupied. I didn't dare take a single step.

"That's her, I was sure of it," said the man. "I'm mistaken." He lifted another lid and said, "Look at this one."

Marie let out a scream that echoed from vault to vault. She had recognized her sister. I forgot my fear. She lifted the young girl in her arms and spoke to her as if she could answer and understand. I wanted to take Marie out of there.

"No, leave me. I won't let her go. Augustine! My sister, answer me. You're not dead. Our mother is in Paris. She would die if she saw you. Wake up!" She shook the corpse, its head going in all directions. It was horrible to witness. I can never erase this scene from my memory. Without the budding breasts that showed her to be female, I would not have recognized Augustine at all. Her body was covered in big, black splotches, and her hair was cut short so she looked like a boy. I couldn't snap out of my surprise. I signaled to the guard to separate Marie from her sister. Marie wailed in her grief.

"Come now," I said, "don't disturb the rest of the dead. You shouldn't cry near them. Come into the chapel." I steered her out of the mortuary, despite her resistance.

I asked where Augustine had died, and I was taken

to the Saint-Marie ward. I wanted to know what had made her ill. A nun came up and asked me if I was the parent of no. 15. I remembered that in Saint-Louis, I had had this same number. I answered no, that I had come with her sister.

The nun pulled me into a corner and said, "I wouldn't tell you in front of a parent how this poor girl was brought to us. She had been picked up by the police at the gate of the École. She'd been forced to drink. She was found in the middle of a brawl. She'd been beaten, and she was black with bruises. She was brought here.

"They said she had an infection, and I cut her hair. She gave me your address, saying that she was a servant in your household. Fever took her, and she died at four o'clock that day. Console her sister. I believe that the merciful God had mercy for the poor girl in taking her."

We went downstairs. They asked if we would bury her or if we would have her entombed. I paid thirty francs. I pulled Marie away.

Marie, out of her mind with grief, wanted to locate her mother and tell her to meet us the next day at ten o'clock at the Hotel Dieu, to see her daughter Augustine, who was very ill.

This scene was even worse than the day before. The mother waited for us at the door of the hospital. She said to Marie, "You didn't tell me the name of Augustine's ward."

I said quietly to Marie that I'd brought the linen for her sister to speed up the preparations. I'd do my best to buy her some time.

An orderly came down by another staircase and, once he was near us, said to me, "Madame, would you like to see the young girl before she's nailed in? That's the usual thing, to make sure someone doesn't do anything to the body."

"Who are you nailing in?" said Marie's mother, and she followed the orderly before I could stop her. The lid was set when we arrived.

"Where is my daughter? Is she the one you wanted to carry off?" She threw herself onto the man as he worked, pushed him away, and tore her nails to lift the planks. The men moved aside because she had the right to see the dead. She moved the cloth and recognized her daughter, then she fell onto her. The orderlies lifted her, but she fought them. They laid her on a mattress on the floor. Marie made as if to lift her sister and begged me not to leave her mother, who sometimes had epileptic seizures. She was having an attack at that very moment.

When their mother regained consciousness, I took her out before she could remember anything. Marie would remember everything for her.

❧

I shut myself off in order to not see these faces in tears. It all upset me; my pulse was racing. I had to send for the doctor. He ordered many things, including rest and strong doses of digitalis syrup. I didn't do half of what he prescribed me. Instead of resting, I spent nights lying awake. Winter came, and I fell more seriously ill. I had to be taken care of. I took to bed.

One night I was thinking of Robert, and my heart beat at his memory. I mechanically picked up the bottle of tincture of digitalis. Instead of drinking the few drops that always calmed me, I swallowed it all. This terrified me. I always told the doctor that I regularly followed his orders, but here I was doing no such thing. He didn't grasp the weaknesses inherent in his practice.

The gossip was that I wasn't going out, that I had been hit hard by the death of Lise. People who came to see me, not knowing the state of my heart, attributed my depression to her death. There was maybe some truth in what my friends said, but it wasn't the only thing. All these unhappy endings all around me brought me down. I couldn't sleep without seeing this phantasmagoria of dreams enlarged by fever and grief. Soon enough, I stopped resisting. Soon enough, I took in the horrors bit by bit, and I struggled bravely along with it. But all this existential exhaustion didn't make me any prettier.

I knew that Robert had rented a house to Zizi at Saint-James. Though he had broken up with her, he had always cared for her, and he still looked out for her future. I asked myself what this woman had done to be so lucky,

One day, while sitting by a large fire in my room, I did my best to warm my body and my spirit again. A ring of the bell made the flame sputter. Marie must have been out, because a second ring sounded, louder than the first. I got up in a bad mood at being bothered, saying, "Who is ringing so insistently? I would only forgive one person in the world for this."

22.

The Countryside

I OPENED THE DOOR AND stood there like a stone.

"Is it so terrible," said Robert, "that a tall young man has come along with me? I'm going to start again. We're frozen!"

I didn't move from my spot, I was so seized up. I left the two of them standing on the tile in the hallway.

Robert took me in his arms, kissed me, and brought me into my room. "Oh, good! There's a fire, so we're not going to be kicked out without warming up. It seems that we're not welcome. I present to you one of my neighbors in the country, one of my best friends, Martin. I brought him to meet you, hoping that you would make us welcome. I beg your pardon, my dear Martin, if I was mistaken."

At last the power speech returned to me. "You're

correct to count on my being happy to see you and on my welcoming you and your friend. I was shocked by your abrupt arrival. I'm sorry it took me so long to recover myself, but I was not expecting you at all!"

"Good, good," said Robert. "If it's only that, then it's nothing. How are you?"

"Better, now that I've seen you."

He looked at me sideways and said, "You'll dine with us tonight? I'm staying in Paris for three days, and I'm hiding out at your place. Do you still see Frisette? We must invite her so Martin isn't too bored. I have so much to tell you. It's been six months since I've seen you. Do you still love me at least a little?"

He saw the answer in my eyes.

"Someone is ringing," he said laughing. "If it's my replacement, I'm telling you now I'm going to meet him at the door."

It was actually Jean, who knew of Robert. Robert breezily ushered him in, offered him a seat, did him the honors of my home, gave orders like the master of the house. Poor Jean looked to be the most miserable of men. He had no idea how to extract himself from this scene. I stood near the fireplace, very embarrassed by my own attitude. At last Jean fled as if he'd only come to pay me a visit as a friend. Robert laughed like a madman.

I forced myself to be friendly to Martin. Being nice to those around Robert seemed like good politics. That evening, I treated him like one of my conquests. After dinner, I left the room to talk to the servant, but I needed to know what Martin was going to say about me. I couldn't resist the temptation—I listened at the door.

"How do you like her?" said Robert.

"Very much," answered Martin. "I like her much better

than the one whose house you took me to yesterday. This one has brains. The other is stupid."

"It's true," said Robert, "she is embarrassing."

Curiosity killed the cat, and yet again, the proverb did not lie. He'd gone to another woman's house before coming to mine. He was giving this country mouse a tour of his mistresses. I didn't want to admit that I had been listening, but I couldn't hide the change that came over me. Robert looked at me more often without comprehending why I attacked him with pinpricks.

"What's happened, Celeste? You're acting funny."

"I am funny? It's you who are funny. You brought back from your Berry I don't know what kind of country manners. You drop into my house like a bomb, you meet my friend at the door, and you say that I'm funny! I think you can behave like this at Madame Zizi's, since she's your first choice, but with me it's fine! No shame."

He didn't answer. He looked at Martin, thinking that he had let something slip. The poor boy, who was timidity itself, raised both his hands and answered with a look that said, *I swear to you, I said nothing!*

Robert couldn't help laughing at Martin's naivete. He told me that, since they'd arrived in the middle of the night and he didn't own my place, he had gone to the house he owned. I didn't argue, but I liked him less.

The least bit of contrariness gave me palpitations, and I coughed up blood. My doctor came the next day, and Robert asked him what I had.

"She has," he said, "a very unwell mind. She doesn't want to listen at all, and she does exactly the opposite of what I tell her. I'm not coming back anymore because she is going from bad to worse. She had a small inflammation, and she has let it grow. It's not dangerous, but it will last a long time if you don't take care of it."

Robert and Martin spoke together. They looked at me and seemed to struggle against an idea. Robert had already delayed his departure by several days.

"I really must go," he told me every morning.

"Leave," I said to him now. "I'm going to get my life back in order to forget you."

"Do you want to kill yourself? That's what'll happen."

"Do as I advise," Martin said to him. "It's all my fault."

"Let's go," said Robert. "I'm not going to beg. Céleste, pack a bag. I'm taking you to the country. We're leaving tonight. I'll conceal you as much as possible. If anyone sees you, they'll assume that you're coming along for Martin."

I couldn't believe my ears. I never asked myself if pity was causing Robert to do something that he would regret. I didn't understand any of it, only that I was the happiest woman. No illness has ever caused so much joy. I turned around and set to work packing my trunk, setting boots on top of flowered bonnets. He laughed to see the happiness that he'd given me. I was lost inside my head. I tried to put my little dog in my bag.

The hour of departure arrived. I took leave of Marie, putting her in charge of my apartment. She began to cry, which was silly.

I wanted to pinch myself to see if I was dreaming, I was so happy. Even if Robert had only brought me along out of pity, I would create some way to make it up to him, thanks to the happiness that was healing me. I went out like the Pont-Neuf of today.

Martin offered me his arm when we disembarked at the stations. He was so chivalrous. Robert came near from time to time so that Martin couldn't take his role too seriously. The railway only went to Vierzon, and it made twenty-five stops on the way to Robert's. He had left his travelling carriage at the apartment, so his valet had hired horses from the post. We climbed into the coupe, Robert and I. Martin, so as not to bother us, took his place on the seat behind with Joseph, the valet.

It had snowed the day before, and it was a blackly cold. Robert closed the windows, and our breath made a curtain against curious onlookers. The driver cracked his whip, and the carriage with its eight springs shook and rolled over the snow as if over a carpet. The wheels didn't make a sound. We went quickly; the trees disappeared like shadows. I began to dream. I thought I was surrounded by ghosts. I could no longer catch hold of reality. I thought I'd fallen asleep. I didn't move out of fear that I'd wake.

The *Thousand and One Nights* were a simple story. What happened to me was a saga, a legend.

Night began to fall. I could no longer see my hallucinations. I felt sick, and we stopped. I closed my eyes, believing my visions had ended. We were at an inn, and lanterns were lit. The driver cursed because he had to ride in the saddle this time, and the roads were bad. I gripped Robert's hands and told him of all the love and gratitude that I had in my heart. Then, falling under the influence of fatigue, I fell asleep on his shoulder.

All of a sudden, he leaned against the door. When I lost the support of his shoulder, I woke with a start.

He called out, "What are you doing, driver? You're taking us back!"

Groans answered him. Robert opened the door and leapt to the head of the horses just as they were about to roll us into a bog. Martin, who had been wrapped up in his cape in the back seat, was asleep next to Joseph. Both climbed down and went to the driver, who lay motionless in the snow twenty paces from the carriage. The unlucky man had fallen, along with the porter. The porter couldn't save the driver or stop the carriage, and it had rolled over his legs. He couldn't move without crying out in pain. We were near another inn, so Robert unhitched a horse and rode off to find help. He returned with an improvised stretcher and a doctor. He gave a few louis to the wounded, and we took off again with another driver.

The emotion, the fatigue, the cold made me numb. I fell asleep, but it was a restless sleep. We were on a bad road, and the carriage jolted and jumped. I strained to see where we were. The night was black, and the trees were closing in above us like a tunnel. We were going at a walking pace, and my eyelids became heavy again.

I felt a jolt and at the same time heard a woman cry, "The gate, please?"

The servant opened the gate, and we rolled on. The moon came out from behind the clouds and lit up a beautiful chateau. The towers were outlined in a deep gray with an imposing and solemn majesty. Snow covered the ground like a shroud. The pine trees were dressed like tombs. It looked like a cemetery with towering headstones. A door opened, and a man came out with a lantern. The horses surrounded us with a cloud of steaming breath.

I was taken into a great room, where the fireplace was eight feet tall. M. Martin was taken to his room in the building to the right. I followed Robert. He went up a stone staircase in a tall tower to the left.

I walked in silence, not daring to breathe. The echo

was menacing. I seemed to see shadows pull free from the walls to come after me. We went into a large bedroom where a servant was lighting a fire. There were four candles lit, and the room was barely illuminated. I saw something that I had no clue about: the splendor of the fifteenth century. This room, which may have been ten meters square, was hung in highly decorated red brocade between the carved and gilded wooden columns. There were beveled mirrors in gorgeous frames and paintings over the doors and fireplaces. The bed was gilded wood and decorated in silk that matched the hangings. A basket of gilded flowers hung from the ceiling, with silk curtains with gold fringe cascading down from it. The furniture was of lacquered and ornamented rose wood. Huge overstuffed armchairs in red and gold completed the furnishings. The bed faced the fireplace.

I was pulled from my examination of the room by awful cries. I didn't know these voices, and I was afraid of them. Robert began to laugh. He told me that at the top of the tower there were owl nests. Often in the night, they made a ruckus. I said that I was angry they were doing so on the day of my arrival. They were naughty birds! The fire crackled in the hearth, the pine resin popped. This made me forget the owls, which were silent the rest of the night.

※

In the morning when I awoke, it took me a while to recognize where I was. A bell rang for lunch. Martin came to find me and take me to the dining room. We crossed the great hall that I'd seen the day before, a billiards room, an enormous salon, and a small salon to arrive at the dining room. After lunch, Martin showed me around. The sun had changed how everything looked compared to last night. A creeping vine enlaced the towers, and the green trees scattered around the grounds cheered up the winter's sadness a little. The chateau was on a hill and had a view of the vast valley. The snow had half melted.

"Let's go see the horses and dogs," said Martin, who was not at all bothered by acting as host. The stables were immaculate and well kept. The first held ten horses, and each stall was furnished for a horse not worth less than three or four thousand francs. All had hoods to cover their heads and capes that were emblazoned with Robert's coat of arms. He took me to see the garage. Six of the most handsome carriages were there. We went out through another courtyard. At the approach of their master, the dogs came to the gate. Never had I seen more beautiful dogs. They were white and red, and they had large, friendly faces that made you want to pet them. We went back inside for supper. I always loved flowers, so I gathered a bunch of violets along the way.

All this was a marvel to me. That I was in such a world! Drivers, grooms, cook, gardener, stableboys, valet, farmgirls, animal handlers, and guards. I said to myself, *My God, it must take a fortune to pay for all this!* I took me four days to see all of it. Robert couldn't continue to live this way if he didn't marry a rich woman. He had come into an inheritance where there were four thousand livres of private income per year, but it was shared six ways. This land, which was his entire fortune, was only worth 25,000 livres, and well administered would add at least two percent. He was in the hands of lenders, who had given him little but to whom he owed a lot. Instead of fighting with these people who had swindled him, he let himself be drawn into new deals. The lenders on the Champs-Elysees always had a beautiful horse that had arrived express from London for Robert. Not being content to write him, they came to find him at home. During my stay, I saw a secondhand store owner from Belgium who made an express trip to Berry. Whenever one shady deal fell through, another would succeed. He had done it all! From the bank where no one ever saw any money to the exchanges where he was the only one to profit. Robert didn't know how to get rid of all these bloodsuckers. I was afraid for him. He ran to his ruin with his eyes closed.

He had seventeen horses. He adored the hunt, and it's still a great pleasure for him. Sometimes he was down, but it never lasted long. He was too emotional to know how to account for things. He was good; however, he had moments of brutality. He said harsh things to me that I should have let drop instead of responding. But I did what I could to avoid making scenes. I did my best to change my habits and take up Robert's.

The first day, I was very upset at having the master of this house walking behind me. But behind me was nothing—when he put himself before me, I no longer dared to eat. They would take my plate from me at the same time as all the others, so when dinner was over, I was famished. We sat at the table for two hours for dinner. One time, I remember, I wanted to take my leave, so I moved to get up. Robert looked at me and said stonily, "Where are you going? The general rule is, you only get up from the table with the master of the house." I turned crimson. During the day, when a farmer would come, or a countryman on business, Robert sent me away, saying, "Shut yourself in your room. I don't need the whole world to see you."

One day I received a letter from Marie that said:

Madame would do well to return. She was ill when she left Paris, and everyone is saying that she died. Many of your friends have come by to see if it's true.

I spoke of this to Robert, who was in a bad mood. He said, "Fine! Leave. You're in good health. What the hell do you want to do with yourself? See your friends from Mabille? I like to think that you hold them in little esteem."

"That's where you're wrong. It little matters to me what my friends might be—from Mabille or anywhere else. If they think of me, I am grateful for it. Come on, Robert, be honest. You brought me here, and you regret it. You would like me to leave. I'll go tomorrow."

It was bold of me to say this, but in the depths of my soul, I hoped that he would refuse. He accepted. I thought that, the next day, he would hold me back.

But the next day, he was upset. "I don't regret having brought you here, Céleste; however, you'd better go. I played a dangerous game for fun. I love you very much, but I have to get married. One of my parents wrote to me about it. That's the reason I'm letting you go. I'll write you. We'll be good friends."

My heart was about to burst, but I knew that he was right.

I was taken the next day to Chateauroux with my luggage, and he rode with me into town. When the carriage went through the gate, all my courage left me. I wanted to ask his forgiveness, to beg him to take it back.

God, how I suffered along that road! At the station, I took a seat in a carriage with service to Vierzon. I could no longer hold back my tears. Robert kissed me and left me abruptly. But before he turned away, I had time to see his tear-filled eyes.

What a contrast between my return and the voyage that I'd made some weeks before. I'd been under the spell of joyful love and satisfied vanity, followed by the coldest, the bitterest, the most relentless deception. There are joys that must not be felt when you know you must lose them. There are horizons it is better to not seek when you're obliged to bid them farewell. This grand life that he had been so kind to extend should never have been mine. Ironically, the spell allowed me to steal some moments of happiness, but it gave me only temporary joy and left me with eternal regrets. It was a mirage he had made. I sank back into the mediocre reality of my bohemian life. Instead of this splendid carriage, where I had rolled so sweetly on the soft cushions beside him, I was alone and jolted about in a rough carriage. In one fell swoop, I had lost what made me happy and proud.

Today, years separate me from these emotions. I am able to experience them at ease. When these abrupt changes don't completely rip your heart open, they lift it up and make it stronger. They give you a strength within yourself that you'll later call on to serve others.

I suffered all the more because I saw my situation clearly. I didn't spin out of control, and I kept my good sense. I didn't want Robert, but the idea of another woman going to set herself up at his side burned me like a red-hot iron. I told myself, *If he loved me, he would be less ambitious. He would keep me! And he did cry when I left. If he loves me, he'll come back to me.*

I had arrived at the train. My reasoning wasn't enough to calm me down, and I went on feeling absolutely awful.

All of Paris said I was dead. Adolphe, back from Metz, where he had been since we broke up, had come to my house defeated and ashen. He entered my salon without speaking to Marie and talked to my portrait.

"Is it true, poor girl, that I'll never see you again? I returned too late!"

Marie said, "Too late? Why too late, monsieur?"

"To see Céleste before she died. I loved her so much! I love her still."

"I know why Monsieur thinks that," Marie said, "but Madame is in good health. She's in the country and wrote to me yesterday." He embraced her in his joy and left, leaving his address.

I had just moved back into my house when an officer from the Madeleine quarter came to inquire about me. He was told I wasn't there. He backed off, muttering and saying that he'd find me. Marie told me about it.

I bounced back soon enough. I always had such a passion for living inside me, such a strong lifeforce, that I couldn't remain long in a state of anxiety or depression. I worked on myself until I was back in balance. If suffering became the state of my soul, it would drive me mad or I'd kill myself.

I decided to leave town, to take a trip. I went to the commissioner of my quarter. I got a passport with two witnesses, and I told Jean that I wanted to go to le Havre. I asked him to come along with me. He accepted. My passport, with entry to le Havre, was a guarantee that I would not be punished if I was arrested. I could prove that I had been approved to travel.

We left the same night.

www.ingramcontent.com/pod-product-compliance
Lightning Source LLC
Chambersburg PA
CBHW021147160426
43194CB00007B/718